English for academic study:

Extended writing & research skills

Course Book

Joan McCormack
and John Slaght

Garnet
EDUCATION

University of
Reading

Credits

Published by
Garnet Publishing Ltd.
8 Southern Court
South Street
Reading RG1 4QS, UK

This edition first published 2005.
Reprinted with corrections 2006.

ISBN 1 85964 746 4

British Cataloguing-in-Publication Data
A catalogue record for this book is available from the British Library.

Production

Project manager:	Richard Peacock
Project consultant:	Rod Webb
Editor:	Lucy Thompson
Art director:	David Rose
Design:	Mike Hinks
Illustration:	Mike Hinks
Photography:	Corbis: Adrian Arbib, Yann Arthus-Bertrand, Goldberg Diego, Peter Guttman, Martin Jones-Ecoscene, Robert Landau, David Lawrence, Stephanie Maze, Reuters, Norbert Schaefer.

Printed and bound
in Lebanon by International Press

The authors and publishers wish to acknowledge the following use of material:

W. M. Adams, Andrew Jordan & Tim O'Riordan, ed. P. Cloke et. al., *Introducing Human Geographies*, Arnold, 1999, Reproduced by permission of Hodder Arnold.

Contemporary International Relations, Papp, D., © Pearson Education. Reprinted by permission of Pearson Education, Inc.

Extract from 'Safety in Numbers' by A. Barnett and 'Can LA Kick the Car Habit' by Dan Thisdell reproduced with permission from *New Scientist*.

'*Banking System Developments in the Four Asian Tigers*' by Chan Huh, reprinted from the Federal Reserve Bank of San Francisco *Economic Letter* 97–22. The opinions expressed in this article do not necessarily reflect the views of the management of the Federal Bank of San Francisco, or of the Board of Governors of the Federal Reserve System.

Leisure and Tourism, Youell, R. © Pearson Education Limited. Reprinted by permission of Pearson Education, Inc.

Crown copyright material is reproduced with the permission of the Controller of HMSO and the Queen's Printer for Scotland.

Core Geography, Naish et al. © Pearson Education Limited. Reprinted by permission of Pearson Education, Inc.

An Introduction to Sustainable Development, 1999, Routledge.

'Reducing Automobile Dependence' © Peter Newman, reproduced by permission of the author.

'Compiling a blibliography' © Mellanie Hodge, 2004.

Contents

1 Introduction to the skills of extended writing and research   Page   5

2 Using evidence to support your ideas   Page   13

3 Structuring your project and finding information   Page   23

4 Developing your project   Page   40

5 Developing a focus   Page   49

6 Introductions, conclusions and definitions   Page   55

7 Incorporating data and illustrations   Page   66

8 Preparing for presentations and editing your work   Page   76

a Appendices   Page   84

Acknowledgements

The creation of these materials stemmed from the need to help international students develop the study skills necessary to function effectively on academic courses in a university context. The rationale behind the material is that students need to develop the confidence and competence to become autonomous learners in order to successfully carry out research and complete assignments, such as extended pieces of written work or oral presentations.

The development of these materials has been a collaborative effort which goes far beyond the collaboration between the authors. The material has evolved over several years of pre-sessional teaching at the Centre for Applied Language Studies at the University of Reading. There have been significant additions from a number of teachers, who have either contributed ideas or given extensive feedback on the materials. The number of teachers involved is too large for us to mention each one individually, but they are all fully appreciated.

In something like their present form, the materials have been trialled on successive pre-sessional courses at the University of Reading since 2001. This trialling has involved almost a thousand students, and they too have provided feedback in terms of course evaluation, as well as with their responses to the tasks in the programme. We very much appreciate the contribution of students whose work has been adapted and incorporated into the materials.

We would particularly like to thank Jill Riley for her meticulous editing and typing up of the materials and Corinne Boz and Bruce Howell for their very significant contributions to the development of the accompanying on-line tasks.

Joan McCormack and John Slaght, Authors, March 2005

1 Introduction to the skills of extended writing and research

In this unit you will be introduced to extended writing and informed about the projects you will work on in this book.

Academic disciplines on the typical university campus

There are a number of schools (or faculties) that exist on university campuses, and within these there are also departments and units (or sections). Students often have to produce a specific type of work in order to be assessed, depending on the school, faculty, department or unit they are studying in. The type of writing that students have to do also depends on the level of study: whether undergraduate or postgraduate.

Extended writing at university: Why do students write?

Students write for a number of purposes, according to the particular requirements of their course. In many cases the topic or title will be predetermined by the lecturer, and may require the reading of recommended texts. At other times, for example, when writing a thesis or dissertation, students have to choose their own titles. The students will receive support and guidelines from a supervisor, but on the whole they are expected to work independently at this level.

The reasons why students carry out extended academic writing activities may include:

- to develop and express their ideas;
- to provide evidence to support their ideas;
- to dispute or support existing theories;
- to display knowledge.

The type of writing required by students will be determined by the purpose of the writing.

Task 1: What do students write?

You are going to brainstorm some ideas about the kind of writing students have to do at university. This means you are going to write down some ideas about this topic. You are going to do this very quickly within a time limit, so don't worry about the accuracy of your grammar or spelling.

1.1 List the kinds of writing students have to do at university, without worrying about the order.

1.2 Note your ideas in the box below; one idea has been written for you.

WHAT STUDENTS HAVE TO WRITE AT UNIVERSITY

- *Reports of experiments*
-
-
-
-
-
-
-
-
-
-
-
-

University students are often asked to write *essays*. These may be as short as 600 words, especially during examinations. However, undergraduates as well as postgraduates are also frequently required to write *extended essays*. A typical length for an extended essay might be 3,000 words. We sometimes refer to these extended essays as *projects*.

However, not all students write traditional-style essays. For example, in the Engineering Department of a university, students will often be expected to write *reports* on projects they have been working on during their course. Towards the end of their period of study, the same students will probably be expected to write a *thesis*. This is 'a long piece of writing based on your own ideas and research as part of a university degree, especially a higher degree such as a PhD' (Cobuild 1993 *Advanced Learner's Dictionary*). Sometimes this is called a *dissertation* – 'a long formal piece of writing on a particular subject, especially for a university degree' (Cobuild 1994 *Advanced Learner's Dictionary*). In the United Kingdom and Ireland, a dissertation is written for a Master's-level degree.

In certain academic disciplines, such as Applied Linguistics, Education or Sociology, students may be required to write a *case study*. A good example of a case study might be the 'study of speech, writing, or language use of one person, either at one point in time or over a period of time, e.g., a child over a period of one year' (Richards, Platt & Weber, 1985). A student in an Applied Linguistics Department would probably write a case study like this.

Students also have to write *notes*: from written sources, or when attending a lecture, seminar or tutorial. Some students annotate lecture handouts, either by highlighting key points or writing notes/comments in the margins of the text, which may be useful later.

Task 2: Types of writing

Complete the following table to help your understanding of the types of writing described above.

Type of writing	Type of student	Explanation
Essay		A traditional 600–6,000 word text written as an assignment or for an exam
Extended essay or project		
Report	Undergraduate/ postgraduate	
Thesis		
Dissertation		
Case study		An account that gives detailed information about a person, group or thing and their development over a period of time

Whatever form of extended writing students are expected to do, the process will usually involve the following steps:

- gathering information from various sources;
- organising this information so that it appropriately answers the needs of the task that the writer has to complete;
- planning the text;
- drafting and redrafting the text until it communicates the information and ideas fully and clearly.

Students are expected to take responsibility for working through these steps. In other words, they should work independently to a large extent.

Types of assessment

The writing of reports, theses, dissertations and case studies is all part of the assessment process in most academic disciplines in the majority of universities. Another form of assessment is through *oral presentations*. Presentations are normally given as part of a study project. For example, a student writing a report might give a presentation in order to 'present' his or her report in a clear, concise way.

Oral presentations can be given by an individual student, or they can be group presentations. Another form of presentation is the *poster presentation*. In this case, the student prepares a visual display outlining the work or project he/she has been involved in. A poster presentation will normally be displayed during a student *conference*. Students display their work, and participants and visitors to the conference are invited to look at the display and ask the author of the poster questions about the process or information they can see. At the same time, other students will normally be giving oral presentations at the conference.

Apart from the methods of written and oral assessment mentioned above, of course, students will probably have to take exams at the end of term and/or the end of year, as well as at the end of their university studies when they take their *final examinations*.

Writing projects

You will do most of the extended writing in this course independently, outside the classroom. Any writing that goes on in the classroom will normally be for editing purposes, when you will have an opportunity to consult your tutor and redraft your work accordingly. You will be expected to follow a *process writing* approach (see *English for academic studies: Writing*, Course Book pp 7–8 for a full explanation of this term). This approach includes editing your work, submitting your first draft, and redrafting the project after your tutor has given you feedback.

You might also have the opportunity to take part in one-to-one tutorials with your tutor, in order to discuss your first and subsequent drafts. You will be expected to go on redrafting and revising the content of your text in order to improve it, as long as you are able to submit your final draft before any submission deadline. The final product is less important than the process you go through while writing it. Writing your project gives you the opportunity to practise the academic skills and conventions you have been learning and developing on your pre-sessional course.

The project you are going to complete will be on the topic of *sustainable development*. For this project, you will be given certain 'core' texts to consult. However, you will have the opportunity to carry out some independent research, because you can select *two extra texts* of your own choice from books, journals or online sources. You will need to provide hard copies of these sources for your tutor.

The aim of this project is to give you practice in finding appropriate information. Although a range of texts is available, you will need to read 'selectively' in order to find information that is relevant to the task title. You will also practise note-taking from these sources and then summarising your notes effectively. You will be given advice on how to avoid plagiarism and how to acknowledge the origin of your information.

The project in this book should be considered as practice for a second project. For the second project, you should make all the decisions about subject, topic and title, and you will carry out the research independently (including the search for appropriate sources).

At each stage of both projects, you should make best use of any tutorial sessions you may have. University staff are busy people and expect you to come with readily prepared questions and a thorough knowledge of the work you have been carrying out. Preparation for tutorials is your responsibility.

Task 3: Analysing the task

Before beginning any task, it is important to analyse the requirements of the task so that you have a very clear idea of your purpose for writing.

Consider the following project title:

To what extent can the problems of urbanisation be met by a policy of sustainable development?

Discuss the following with a partner:

a) Look at the project title above and highlight the key words/phrases.

b) How is the title framed (e.g. statement/question/heading)?

c) What does the title ask you to do?

Task 4: The stages of writing a project

There are three stages in producing an extended essay or project: **planning, researching** and **writing up**. In each of these stages there are a number of smaller steps.

4.1 Put the steps listed below into the appropriate stages on page 10 (*Planning, Researching* or *Writing up*), in the most appropriate order. Write the steps in full; do not write numbers. Note that one step can be placed in two stages.

a) Read the first draft.

b) Edit the draft – decide objectively whether your ideas have been expressed clearly.

c) Think of a working title for the project. ✓

d) Search for relevant journals/books/information in the library and on the Internet.

e) Write down the details of your sources.

f) Decide if you need to do more reading.

g) Write the contents page, bibliography, title page and abstract. ✓

h) Arrange a tutorial with your tutor.

i) Do some reading.

j) Decide on a topic.

k) Write the first complete draft.

l) Highlight/take notes of relevant information. ✓

m) Plan the contents in detail.

n) Work on establishing a clear focus.

o) Make a rough outline plan of your ideas.

p) Check that sources are available/accessible.

Planning

1. _____

2. _____

3. _Think of a working title for the project._

4. _____

5. _____

6. _____

Researching

1. _____

2. _____

3. _Highlight/take notes of relevant information._

4. _____

5. _____

Writing up

1. _____

2. _____

3. _____

4. _____

5. _Write the contents page, bibliography, title page and abstract._

4.2 Discuss your answer with another student. There is more than one possible order for the steps.

Task 5: Starting Project 1

In Task 3, you analysed the title of the project: *To what extent can the problems of urbanisation be met by a policy of sustainable development?*

You are now going to work on this project by answering the following questions, which are grouped under the three broad headings *Introduction*, *Main body* and *Conclusion*. First read the questions.

Introduction

a) What is 'sustainable development'? (Definition)

b) What is 'urbanisation'? (Definition)

c) What are the problems of urbanisation? (Background information)

d) What policies of sustainable development exist or could be introduced? (Background information)

e) To what extent do you <u>think</u> sustainable development can solve the problems?
[The expression '*To what extent*' allows you to give your opinion about the likely success of sustainable development policies. Your position (opinion) on this question will help form your 'thesis' – that is the main argument you will present in your project.]

Main body

f) What specific problems are related to the lack of urban space?
What evidence can you find for this?

g) What specific problems are related to urban transport?
What evidence can you find for this?

h) What are the possible solutions to the problems outlined above?

i) What evidence can you find to suggest that a policy of sustainable development can be successful?

Conclusion

j) Based on the evidence you have presented above, to what extent can a policy of sustainable development meet the current urban problems related to a lack of space and transport?

k) Does the evidence you put together in the 'main body' support the thesis you introduced in your introduction?

In the appropriate boxes on the next page, brainstorm some ideas on the above questions. At the moment, you are only being asked to guess what the answers *might* be. After this, you will have to do some reading to find out whether your guesses are correct or not. You will also be reading to find out other ideas about the topic. This reading stage is one of the most important parts of your work because you will be looking for *evidence* to support your ideas.

Write your initial ideas in the boxes overleaf. You only need to write in note form.

Introduction

1. _____
2. _____
3. _____
4. _____
5. _____
6. _____

Main body

1. _Lack of playground facilities for children._
2. _____
3. _____
4. _____
5. _____
6. _____

Conclusion

1. _____
2. _____
3. _____
4. _____
5. _____
6. _____

2 Using evidence to support your ideas

In this unit you will:
- discuss the importance of providing evidence in academic writing;
- learn different methods of incorporating sources;
- practise summarising information.

Introduction

It is part of Western academic convention that any claim made in writing, e.g. an opinion or generalisation, is supported by evidence. You need to show some 'proof' that what you are saying is correct. You need to support any statements or points you make with 'evidence'. This gives your work more academic 'weight'. This is a very important part of Western academic convention.

Using the ideas of other people in your text and acknowledging them is an essential part of academic writing. This means referring to them twice, both within the text itself, as well as in a bibliography at the end.

In academic writing, and especially in the early stages, students are not expected to write their own original ideas. In fact, university departments often require students to produce written work in order to demonstrate that:

- they have read, understood and evaluated some of the literature in their field;
- they can synthesize ideas from more than one source;
- they can select appropriate academic sources to support their point of view or perspective.

Reading list

To carry out your first project successfully, you should make use of the following *reading list*. The printed *sources* are available in Appendix 4.

Bibliography

- Adams, W.M. (1999) 'Sustainability' in Cloke P. et al. (eds) *Introducing Human Geographies*. London: Arnold, pp. 125–129

- Bilham-Boult, A. et al. (1999) *People, Places & Themes*. Oxford: Heinemann pp. 202–205; p. 208

- Chaffey, J. (1994) 'The Challenge of Urbanisation' in Naish & Warn (eds) *Core Geography* London: Longman, pp.138-146

- Elliot, J.A. (1999) 'Sustainable Urban Livelihoods' in *An Introduction to Sustainable Development*. London: Routledge, pp. 151–153

- Newman, P. (1999) 'Transport: Reducing Automobile Dependence' in Satterwaite D. (ed) *The Earthscan reader in Sustainable Cities*: Earthscan Publications, pp. 67–92

- Thisdell, D. (June 1993) *Can L.A. Kick the Car Habit? New Scientist* pp. unknown

- UK Government: 08/10/04 *Sustainable development: the UK government's view* http://www.sustainable-development.gov.uk viewed 12/03/03

- Wikipedia Encyclopaedia 23/11/03 *Urbanization* http://en.wikipedia.org/wiki/urbanization viewed 19/12/03

Task 1: Selective reading

In Task 3 of Unit 1 you analysed the title of the project (page 9). The next stage is to look at sources relevant to your title.

With a partner, discuss the following questions:

a) Why are you going to read the sources in the reading list?

b) How are you going to read them?

c) What are you going to do as you read?

One of the most important things to remember about an academic assignment, whether you are preparing to write a long dissertation or a simple summary for an oral presentation, is that you are expected to frame your ideas 'in your own terms'. This means that your reader expects to read about *your* point-of-view. However, you must support your point of view with evidence from the *literature* (in this case, the sources you have read from the reading list above), or from your fieldwork (e.g. collecting data) or experiments. By supporting *your* opinion with ideas and information from the literature, you are strengthening your viewpoint and therefore providing a more *compelling* argument. Such *evidence* is expected in academic writing.

Therefore, your purpose for reading the sources listed above is to find information (evidence) that is relevant to your idea or *thesis* about the topic. It is important to remember that not all of the information in the sources you have will be relevant. Therefore, you will have to read *selectively* in order to identify the relevant information. It is important to develop the skill of selective reading now, because during your academic course you will be expected to read literally hundreds of pages every week. Students are often shocked when they begin their studies by the amount of reading they have to do. One strategy for dealing with this heavy reading load is to become good at selective reading.

Before you look at the texts in the reading list, you will look at some examples of how evidence is incorporated into academic writing and carry out some practice tasks.

Task 2: Incorporating evidence into academic work

2.1 Look at the examples below. Which statement would you take more seriously? Give a reason for your answer.

a) The number of tourists has increased considerably in the last year.

b) The number of tourists has increased by 10% since last year, according to the most recent government report on the economy (Government Statistics 2001).

2.2 Now look at the following examples of how evidence is used to support a point. Underline the point being supported, and circle the evidence given.

a) Any discussion of financial markets must begin with a definition of what they are:

'A financial market is the place or mechanism whereby financial assets are exchanged and prices of these assets are set' (Campbell, 1988).

b) According to Wang (2001), education is the key aspect underlying the successful economic development in a society.

c) Djabri states that operations research is the application of the methods of science to complex problems (Djabri, 2001).

d) As Sloman (1999) has demonstrated, there are two main methods of measuring unemployment.

e) This antibiotic has an immediate effect on the illness (Braine, 1997).

When incorporating evidence into academic writing:

- You can use **direct quotations**; this means you use the exact words of the writer, and use inverted commas or italics. You must acknowledge the writer (see a) above).

- You can **paraphrase or summarise** the writer's ideas. This means you express the author's ideas, using your own words as much as possible. You must acknowledge the writer. You do not include any ideas that are not included in the original (see b), c), d) and e) above).

In most academic writing, the incorporation of evidence is done by using a mixture of the above. You might summarise ideas generally, while acknowledging the sources, and occasionally use a direct quotation if this seems to encapsulate the point you wish to make. You might choose to refer *directly* to your source (see b), c) and d) above), using appropriate language. Or you might simply refer *indirectly* to the source by putting the name and date after your statement (see e) above).

Task 3: Referencing

3.1 In order to get some practice in identifying ways of referencing, read the following extract from the text: 'Environmental problems and management' by Andrew Jordan & Tim O'Riordan (1999), and highlight the references.

ENVIRONMENTAL PROBLEMS AND MANAGEMENT

The origins of environmental policy

Recognition of the need to both transform and adjust to nature is a fundamental aspect of the human condition. While we may think of 'the environment' as a modern political issue that gained popular appeal in the 1960s, the roots of environmentalist thinking stretch back far into the past (O'Riordan, 1976). The natural environment provides humanity with the material resources for economic growth and consumer satisfaction. But throughout history there have always been social critics and philosophers who have felt that humans also need nature for spiritual nourishment and aesthetic satisfaction. John Muir, the redoubtable founder of the Sierra Club in the USA, felt that without wild places to go to humanity was lost:

> **Thousands of tired, nerve-shaken over-civilized people are beginning to find out that going to the mountains is going home; that wilderness is a necessity and that mountain parks and reservations are fountains not only of timber and irrigating rivers, but as fountains of life. Awakening from the stupefying effects of over-industry and the deadly apathy of luxury, they are trying as best they can to mix their own little ongoings with those of Nature, and to get rid of rust and disease ... some are washing off sins and cobwebs of the devil's spinning in all-day storms on mountains.** *(quoted in Pepper, 1984:33)*

Environmental protection is justified in remarkably similar terms today. What is dramatically different is the *extent* of popular concern. The critical question which needs to be asked is *why did modern environmentalism blossom as a broad social movement spanning different continents in the late 1960s and not before?* There is strong evidence that environmental problems like acidification and pesticide pollution materially worsened and became more widespread in the public mind in the 1960s and 1970s. The American sociologist Ronald Inglehart (1977), however, believes that we also have to look to society for an explanation. On the basis of careful and intensive public opinion analysis he argues that modern environmentalism is the visible expression of a set of 'new political' values held by a generation of 'post-materialists' raised in the wealthy welfare states of the West. This liberated class no longer had to toil to supply their material needs and set out to satisfy what the psychologist Maslow (1970) terms its 'higher order' requirements like peace, tranquillity, intellectual and aesthetic satisfaction. This was surely a 'post-materialist' sensibility, but at first it was confined to a vociferous minority that tried to push their values onto the majority who steadfastly regarded themselves more as consumers than as citizens.

Other commentators, however, highlight the tendency for environmental concern to exhibit a cyclical pattern over time, with particularly pronounced peaks in the late 1960s and late 1980s. Closer scrutiny reveals that these short-term 'pulses' coincided with periods of economic growth and social instability, which at first blush seems consistent with Inglehart's thesis. Other sociologists have also observed that materially richer and better educated sections of society tend to give much higher priority to environmental protection than poorer ones, with the highest rates among those working in the 'non-productive' sectors of the economy, such as education, health and social care (Cotgrove and Duff, 1980). Conversely, concern tends to tail off during periods of economic recession (Downs, 1972), and is not normally as pronounced in poorer sections of Western society or in developing countries. The birth of the modern environmental movement in the late 1960s certainly coincided with a period of economic prosperity and societal introspection. Whether this led to or was caused by the accumulating evidence of environmental decay is open to interpretation.

Source: Jordan, A. & O'Riordan, T. (1999): 'Environmental Problems and Management' in: Cloke, Crang, P. & Goodwin, M. (eds) *Introducing Human Geographies*. London: Arnold

3.2 Decide if the references in the text are direct quotations or paraphrases/summaries. Pay attention to the kind of language used. Complete columns 1 and 2 in the table below. The first one has been done for you as an example.

Name and date	Direct/indirect reference	Idea expressed
O'Riordan, 1976	Indirect	E
John Muir		

3.3 In the box below is a list of the ideas expressed in the text. Match them with the appropriate references in the table on page 16. The first one has been done for you as an example.

IDEAS EXPRESSED BY ENVIRONMENTALISTS

A   Once people have fulfilled their basic human needs, they want to achieve a better quality of life.

B   Interest in the environment tends to coincide with the condition of the economic climate.

C   Environmentalism is a way of demonstrating political values.

D   It is essential for the environment to be preserved for the sake of our future.

E   The awareness of environmental issues is not necessarily a modern concept.

F   Only certain privileged sections of society have environmental concerns.

Task 4: Purposeful reading

Any reading you do should have a clear purpose. It should help you find information relevant to the project title, which is **To what extent can the problems of urbanisation be met by a policy of sustainable development?**

As discussed in Unit 1 (page 11), it can be useful to define key terms. In this case, the key terms you are asked to define are *sustainable development* and *urbanisation*. You are now going to try to find definitions of these terms, which you will later incorporate into your project, by visiting the appropriate websites and looking at the texts in Appendix 4 at the back of this book.

4.1 Look at the sources in Appendix 4 at the back of this book and the websites in the reading list. Highlight the text relevant to the definitions. You can do this either by underlining the information, using a highlighter pen or annotating the text by writing a note in the margin.

4.2 Make a careful note of the source of the information (i.e. title and writer) and the page number.

Summarising information from texts

One of the key skills involved in using/referring to sources is summarising; this means being able to state clearly and succinctly the key ideas or thrust of an argument. The summary should be in your own words, with an acknowledgement of the source. If you summarise ideas in the exact words of the original without acknowledging the writer, or fail to name your source, this is considered to be plagiarism – a form of cheating. Universities have strong views about this, which are discussed further below.

How to summarise

- First it is important to decide why you are summarising. Are you going to use this information in an essay? Do you need only the main ideas or are the details also important? Perhaps only sections of the text are relevant; in which case you need to be even more selective.

- Before you attempt to summarise, it is essential that you understand the material you plan to summarise; if the ideas in the material are not clear to you, then they will not be clear to the reader when you express them in writing.

- It is useful to take notes. The first reason for this is to clearly identify the main points of the text, and the second reason is to use these as the basis for writing your summary.

- Write your summary using your own notes as a stimulus – put the original text away. If you follow the text, it will make it more difficult to summarise in your own words.

- When you have finished your summary, you may want to read the original text again in order to ensure you have all the information you need.

When summarising, use the N.O.W. approach:

- **N**OTE down key points
- **O**RGANISE the points
- **W**RITE your summary using these points

Task 5: Features of a summary

Which of the features below do you think characterise a good summary?

5.1 Discuss in pairs or small groups.

5.2 Make a note of your ideas so that you can justify your reasons to the whole class.

A   Using the same order of facts and ideas as the original

B   Using all the information from the original

C   Using none of the same vocabulary as the original

D   Using different grammatical structures from the original

E   Emphasising the points you feel are important in the original

F   Giving your opinion about or commenting on the original text

(Adapted from Trzeciak, J. & Mackay, S.E. (1994) *Study Skills for Academic Writing*, Hemel Hempstead UK: Prentice Hall)

Task 6: Stages in writing a summary

Look at the following short extract from a text on *Environmental Problems and Management*. Imagine you have been asked to:

a) identify the main points;

b) make notes;

c) write a summary based on your notes.

Below is one way of carrying out this assignment.

Stage One: Decide on the purpose for summarising the extract. This is very important because your purpose will determine which particular points you wish to summarise from the text.

Stage Two: Underline the key points. (This is the **NOTE** stage of the summary process.)

> Interest in the environment is not a recent phenomenon; the environment has always affected the growth and development of humankind, both as a source of materials as well as a refuge for the human spirit. The recent interest in protecting the environment is a reflection of both the demand of society for a better quality of life, which may include using the environment as a haven, as well as the need to replenish sources. The difference between the present day and the pre-1960s era is the extent to which concern for the environment has become important; there is much greater interest …

Stage Three: Make a list of the key points in note form, using your own words where appropriate, as shown below. (This is the **ORGANISE** stage of the summary process.)

1: interest in env. = not just recent:. always int. as source of raw materials + 'refuge for human spirit'

2: reasons for recent int. = int. in 'better quality of life' + need to replenish sources of raw materials

3: cf. current interest with pre–1960s = environmental concerns now given more priority

Stage Four: Write the summary based on your notes. (This is the **WRITE** stage of the summary process.)

Sample summary

Man has always had an interest in the environment both as a source of raw materials and as a 'refuge for the human spirit'. Nowadays, the two main environmental interests are based on the concept of a 'better quality of life', as well as the need to replenish the sources of raw materials. In comparison with the pre-1960s, much greater interest in the environment is currently being expressed.

(Jordan, A. & O'Riordan, T. (1999): 'Environmental Problems and Management' in: Cloke, P. Crang, P. & Goodwin, M. (eds.) Introducing Human Geographies. London: Arnold)

Look at the following text, *The Making of Modern Japan*. Your purpose for reading this text is to answer the following question:

What is surprising about modern Japan's current position in the industrialised world?

Follow the **N.O.W.** stages in order to write your summary in two or three sentences.

THE MAKING OF MODERN JAPAN

Modern Japan is a nation of contradictions. Economically powerful and prosperous, its future economic prosperity depends on continued access to reliable sources of external raw materials and stable markets. Militarily constrained because of its U.S.-created constitution, Japan relies on U.S. military strength and the benign intention of others to maintain its security. Pro-Western and modern in its cultural outlook, it reveres old Japanese traditions and customs. The contradictions that exist in Japan – and influence its perceptions of itself and the world – are a product of Japan's historical experiences.

From a global perspective, Japan is a unique nation. With a population half that of the United States and a gross national product 40 percent the size of the United States, Japan must import large percentages of almost every raw material that modern industrialised societies need. Since Japan's evolution to an industrial power did not begin until the late nineteenth century, and since it had no scientific technical tradition, the strides it took to transform itself into a relatively modern industrial state by the beginning of the twentieth century were truly amazing.

Source: Papp, D. (1994) Contemporary International Relations. New York: Macmillan, pp. 325–332

NOTES:

_____

_____

_____

_____

SUMMARY:

_____

_____

_____

_____

Task 8: Practice summary 2

Imagine you are writing the following assignment:

Discuss the causes of the decline of animal species.

8.1　What information could you extract from the text below to help with your assignment?

8.2　Follow the **N.O.W.** approach to write your summary in one or two sentences.

NO SAFETY IN NUMBERS

In the early 18th century flocks of migrating passenger pigeons had darkened the skies over eastern North America, taking three days to pass by. Hunters simply pointed a gun upwards, fired, and then got out of the way as the pigeons tumbled to earth. When the birds stopped to roost, trees broke under their combined weight. With an estimated population of somewhere between 3 and 5 billion, the passenger pigeon was the most abundant bird that ever lived. Yet by the late 1890s the species was almost extinct. A few birds found their way to zoos, but they languished in captivity and refused to breed.

It was a result that perplexed the eminent conservationist, Wallace Craig and his contemporaries, and today's conservationists often face a similar problem. It isn't that living in a zoo can ruin an animal's sex drive. When wild species experience a population crash they can go into free fall, even though you would think that by removing the pressure of over-crowding, the survivors would flourish. New conservationists are beginning to realise that under-crowding itself can help drive species to extinction. It's a counter-intuitive idea, but it's not a new one: the consequences of low population density were first studied more than half a century ago by American biologist Warder Allee.

For decades his ideas were largely forgotten, but now an awareness of these 'Allee effects' looks set to transform conservation practices. "They alter our perception about the risks facing populations that have declined markedly, even if they are not numerically tiny," says Georgina Mace from the Institute of Zoology in London.

Source: Barnett, A. *Safety in Numbers* in *New Scientist* 3 February 2001: Vol 169 No 2276

Task 9: Practice summary 3

From the website sources you are using to write your project, choose TWO sections which are relevant to your project and write a summary similar to the ones you have been practising above.

SUMMARY:

3 Structuring your project and finding information

In this unit you will:
- look at how a project is structured;
- practise writing evaluatively;
- practise selecting information from books and journals;
- practise selecting information from websites.

Task 1: The structure of projects

You are going to look at a project called *Remembering and forgetting: to what extent can we improve memory?* (see Appendix 1) This is quite a good project but it was completed by a student who may have had some more experience of writing projects than you.

First of all, you are going to look at various sections of the project so that you learn some of the vocabulary related to the writing of projects.

1.1 Look at the parts of an academic text listed in the box below. Which of these do you already know about? Discuss them with a partner.

> **A** The conclusion
>
> **B** A quotation
>
> **C** A reference in the text
>
> **D** A subtitle/subheading
>
> **E** The introduction
>
> **F** The bibliography
>
> **G** The first name initials of an author/researcher
>
> **H** The family name of an author/researcher
>
> **I** The main title page
>
> **J** The contents page
>
> **K** A figure or table
>
> **L** Abstract

1.2 Look through the project: *Remembering and forgetting: to what extent can we improve memory?* Label the parts of the text A–L (as on page 23) and discuss in small groups.

How to write an evaluative project

One of the most common problems with projects written by pre-sessional students is that they are too descriptive. It is essential that description should form only part of the project, at most, and that the emphasis should be on the writer's point of view. Project writers should use the information and ideas from their sources to support this *viewpoint*. In order to develop such a position, writers need to think carefully and critically about the content of their sources. Once they have developed a point of view about the topic based on what they have read, writers should select the most appropriate sources to support their viewpoint.

The writer's viewpoint in a text is what may be referred to as his/her *thesis*. In order to write an evaluative, discursive project, the writer should develop a thesis as the starting point and use the sources as the means of supporting this point of view.

Study the following project title, written by a former pre-sessional student:

What can we learn from the restructuring of Korea's banking industry?

The title of this project is written in the form of a question. The answer to this question is what should form the writer's thesis. There are a range of possible answers to the question, 'What can we learn …?' For example, we can learn 'a great deal', 'quite a lot', 'very little' or, in fact, we can learn 'nothing at all'. However, based on an analysis of the sources that he/she has read, the student might decide on the following thesis:

An analysis of the restructuring of the Korean banking system should serve as a model for all banking systems throughout southeastern Asia.

As the student states that the Korean banking system should serve as a 'model', clearly this thesis suggests that 'a great deal' can be learnt from the Korean restructuring exercise. This thesis might also raise the question: Why does the restructuring of Korea's banking system serve as a 'model'? The answer to this question is what should make the project more discursive and analytical. It will not suffice for the writer to describe the Korean banking system, because this will not answer the question 'Why?' What is required is an explanation of the reasons. This may involve a comparison with other banking systems. It will certainly entail an explanation of the features of the Korean banking system that are particularly effective.

It should be clear that a description of the Korean banking system will only form part of the project. The following flow chart may help to clarify this:

Topic: The restructuring of the Korean banking system

↓

Title: What can we learn from the restructuring of Korea's banking industry?

↓

Thesis: The restructuring of the Korean banking system should serve as a model for all banking systems throughout southeastern Asia.

↓

Introduction: Possibly a general summary of all the features of the Korean banking system or a chronological summary of the system's history. The thesis statement usually forms part of the introduction. There may also be an outline of the structure of the project.

↓

Main body: First section: possibly some background information about the Korean banking system that is relevant to the restructuring, e.g. stages at which the restructuring occurred and why it was necessary.

↓

Main body continued: Subsequent sections: an explanation of why each feature of the Korean banking system makes it a 'model', i.e. an analysis of the model. The writer's stance is supported by relevant source references.

↓

Conclusion: Refers back to the thesis statement and draws upon the comments made about all the features described to provide a summative evaluation comment. Possible reference to further analysis that might be carried out on the topic, or a theory about the future of the KBS/banking in southeastern Asia in general.

Reading: Critical reading goes on at every stage of the writing process so that the writer can add to the content.

Text development

Text development

Text development

Text development

Task 2: Descriptive and evaluative writing

Below are four paragraphs related to Korean banking taken from the Federal Reserve Bank of San Francisco website. These paragraphs only form part of the full document, which may be viewed at the website address given at the end of the task.

2.1 Look at the following short text: *Banking System Developments in the Four Asian Tigers*. Identify with a tick (✓) in the table below which paragraphs are mainly descriptive and which show examples of evaluative writing.

Paragraph	Mainly descriptive	Evaluative comments
1		
2		
3		
4		

2.2 Discuss with a partner and underline examples of evaluative writing in the texts.

❶ Over the past 30 years, Hong Kong, Korea, Singapore and Taiwan have had remarkably rapid and sustained economic growth, earning them the nickname the four tigers. Because of the new investment opportunities they provide and because their experiences may offer lessons for less developed economies, they have attracted considerable attention from the financial and policy communities, as well as from economists who have renewed interest in research in theories of economic growth. Despite their physical proximity and shared economic vigour there are some noticeable differences among the tigers. For instance, Hong Kong and Singapore are cities with limited resources, whereas Taiwan and Korea are economies with relatively large populations and more diverse

2. All four economies started out poor in all areas except potential labor supply before they began to grow in the 1960s… Exports from the four economies together made up over 10% of the world's total exports, only slightly less than the US in 1994, compared to only 2.5% in 1971 (Glick and Moreno 1997). The relative shares of imports were about the same. These numbers make it clear that external trade has been an important element in the development of these economies. The external sector (imports + exports), measured relative to total GDP, represented 52% in Korea, 73% in Taiwan, 240% in Hong Kong, and 280% in Singapore in 1994 (for the US, by comparison, it was 17%) …

3. Commercial banks also played a critical role, because they were the major source of private savings. In Korea and Taiwan, the governments required commercial banks to extend credit towards industries targeted in the governments' development plans. Furthermore, due to regulated loan rates, which were below market-determined interest rates, and the lack of loanable funds, these loans were offered at very favorable lending rates …

4. In 1994, the manufacturing sector accounted for about 31% and 27% of GDP in Taiwan and Korea, respectively, whereas banking and financial services accounted for 18% and 17%. In contrast, the relative shares of the manufacturing and financial sectors were 28% and 27% for Singapore and 9% and 27% for Hong Kong. The figures seem to reflect the emphases of the past development policies. "The financial system was rather the accommodator of this real economic performance than its instigator," wrote one economist after examining the role of the financial sector in economic development experiences of these economies (Patrick, 1994). Recent banking sector developments in Korea and, to a lesser extent, Taiwan point to the negative side-effects that government direction of credit to preferred industries can have in the long run. Singapore's experience seems to suggest that a government could implement industrial development policies without directing the credit decisions of the commercial banking sector. Finally, Hong Kong's case seems to illustrate that an active industrial policy may not be essential for rapid economic development.

Chan Huh, Economist

Source: Chan H (1997) 'Banking System Developments in the Four Asian Tigers' Federal Reserve Bank of San Francisco *Economic Letter* 97–22. Viewed 18/05/04 at http://www.frbsf.org/econrsrch/wklyltr/el97-22.html

Task 3: Reading for a specific purpose

As mentioned in Unit 1 Task 1, students are required to read extensively on academic courses. Therefore, it is essential to develop your selective reading skills. The most effective way to do this is to think about your purpose for reading at every stage of your research. For example, if you are looking for a definition to use in the introduction to your project, you should identify the parts of the text that contain this specific information and not worry about the rest of the text at this point.

Now look back at the flow chart on page 25 and decide on the purpose for reading in relation to each section, e.g. one reason for reading might be to look for some *general information* about the Korean banking system in order to make notes for your introduction. Underline other parts of the flow chart related to clear reading purposes.

Reading critically

It is very important to think about what you are reading. Firstly, you need to decide whether what you are reading is useful. Secondly, you should decide if you agree with what is said in the text. You need to relate the information in the text to information that you already know. Are there other texts you have read with similar information that supports or undermines the ideas you are reading? This critical approach to reading is an active skill and helps you interact with the text. This in turn aids your understanding of the text. It also helps you to make important decisions about the text you are reading; for example, whether to skip certain sections of the text, or whether to read a particular section very carefully – you may even decide to make no further use of the text. Interacting with the text and making decisions as you read can save you a great deal of time in the long run.

As you read more about your topic and take relevant notes, you will be able to make connections between ideas that will help you plan and structure your writing. The more you think about what you are reading, the better you will be able to write an evaluative project.

Task 4: Choosing sources

You are now going to decide why the texts in Appendix 4 were chosen for you to refer to when completing your first project.

Make some notes explaining why you think three of the texts have been chosen. Be prepared to compare and discuss your notes. Below are some example notes. Write your notes in the boxes on the next page. Write a full bibliographical reference as the title for each text.

TEXT	Bilham-Boult et al (1999) *People, Places & Themes.* Heinemann
Why it was chosen	• It was published fairly recently – 1999. • It was published by an established publishing company – Heinemann. • It contains various case studies dealing with the problems of urbanisation and how to solve these problems. • Readers can compare the situation in different cities in different parts of the world. This gives them the opportunity to discuss the contents, not simply describe them. • It contains some useful photographs, maps and tables.

TEXT	
Why it was chosen	

TEXT	
Why it was chosen	

TEXT	
Why it was chosen	

Task 5: Finding information

Finding information in textbooks

Many students experience difficulties choosing the most appropriate texts to read when beginning their academic studies, as they seem to have to read so many texts to find the information and ideas they want. Time becomes a real matter of concern as deadlines for completing assignments draw closer. You are more likely to find what you are looking for if you have a clear idea of your purpose, as mentioned before. If you have a clear focus, you can look for the specific type of information you need. Textbooks are one source; you may find several textbooks that interest you, and you can follow a particular procedure to determine how useful each book may be to you. This is the first stage in reading critically.

Check the following first in order to save time:

- **Title**
- **Blurb:** The blurb is the publicity information about the book, written in order to attract people's attention.
- **Table of contents**
- **Index:** An index is an alphabetical list printed at the back of a book, which tells you on which pages important topics are referred to.
- **Date of publication**
- **If it is on the recommended reading list:** This is the list of books (or core texts) that a particular departmental or course lecturer suggests students read for a particular course.
- **Abstract:** If the book has one (see page 31).

5.1 Go to the main library (or your departmental library) and find two books in your subject area.

5.2 Follow the procedure described above (Task 4) for the two books you found. Complete the tables below with details about your books. Your teacher may ask you to do this as homework.

5.3 Based on the information you find, be prepared to report briefly what you have learned about one of the two books to your classmates, e.g. what it is about, who it might be appropriate for, why you would or would not recommend this book for other students in your subject area.

BOOK 1

Subject area	
Title	
Author	
Date of publication	
Intended reader	
Why I would/would not recommend this publication	

BOOK 2

Subject area	
Title	
Author	
Date of publication	
Intended reader	
Why I would/would not recommend this publication	

Finding information in journals

Journals are another source of information, and if you can identify the most appropriate articles, they may provide information about quite a lot of work in the field (subject area). They often have abstracts, which are brief outlines of the main topic of the article. These are extremely useful when you want to identify quickly whether the article is useful for your purposes. The Internet is the most rapidly expanding source of information. You can often find journals online. However, you need to be careful about how you narrow down your search, as otherwise you may find you have far too much information to look through, and again, time can become a problem. You will do some work on online searching later in the course.

Making use of abstracts

An abstract is a short summary of the main points of an academic text. An abstract is also a useful way of identifying whether a text is suitable for your purpose. It is written after the paper has been completed. See the example below. We will look at abstracts in more detail in Units 4 and 8, when you will learn to write your own.

SHOULD ALL MARKETS BE UNDER GOVERNMENT CONTROL?

In general, markets relate to the private sector, and the government does not have the right to interfere in their rules and regulations (Johnston 2002). In spite of this, they often do, which causes controversy. This project attempts to examine the issues involved and to show that the government might be the most appropriate intervening body to regulate markets and to ensure that they function effectively.

Finding information on-line

On-line information is increasingly becoming a source of academic evidence. As there is a greater volume of information available than ever before in this medium, it is essential to be systematic and critical when choosing your sources.

It can be difficult to decide which websites are more likely to be reliable. However, certain websites may be considered to be well researched; for example, websites constructed by educational or government institutions. You can recognise these websites in the following way:

- **.edu** refers to education websites. These are intended to be used as sources for supplementary material for schools, for example, for 'A' level or 'GCSE' students.

- **.ac** refers to academic websites. These are always linked to universities. An example is www.reading.ac.uk/slals/

- **.gov** refers to government websites. These are linked to official government organisations, e.g. http://www.sustainable-development.gov.uk

Other websites may have a commercial interest and can be recognised as follows:

- **.com** and **.org**

A website that contains the ~ symbol (tilde) refers to a personal website. You need to be cautious when using such websites, unless you have a good knowledge of the author.

The explanations in the table below should help you to critically analyse the websites you encounter.

If you cannot find the information outlined below, then you cannot rely on the source, i.e. you may not be able to use it in your work.

Title: • What is the name of the text?	• This will often suggest whether the contents are very specific or if the text gives an overview.
Authority: • Who has written the text? Is the writer a recognised authority, often with several publications, or whose ideas are referred to by other sources? • Is it supported by an organisation you can trust? • Is it possible to check the writer's credentials?	• Sometimes the 'authority' may be an organisation, not an individual. Sometimes the 'authority' is supported by an organisation. It is important that you are able to check this. • If you cannot find the author or organisation responsible for the website, it cannot be used.
Date/currency: • When was the website last updated?	• If the information on the website has not been reviewed appropriately, then it is possible that it is not particularly useful.

Content:	
• What is the text about? • How useful is the text?	• Make sure that it is relevant to your understanding of the topic. • Your evaluation of the content will depend on your reading purpose.
Accuracy: • Does the information appear to be accurate, to the best of your knowledge? • Are there references to other sources? • Are there links to other websites?	• You may be able to check the accuracy of the information in another source. • It is expected that ideas are supported by other sources. • This can often be a way to check the reliability of the website.
Audience: • Who is the intended reader?	• Has the article been written for academics, or at least for readers with a strong interest in the topic, or has it been written for the general reader (like a newspaper article)? You can usually tell the intended audience from the supporting organisation or institution. You can also tell by the style of the language. Does it appear to be formal/neutral, or is it informal? If it appears to be informal, it is unlikely to be a reliable source.

The task below gives some practice in searching for information. There are further practice tasks at **http://www.englishforacademicstudy.com**.

Task 6: Analysing websites

You are now going to practise critically analysing websites. The title of Project 1 is:
To what extent can the problems of urbanisation be met by a policy of sustainable development?

6.1 Use Google® or any other appropriate search engine to find two websites:
one on 'urbanisation' and the other on 'sustainable development'.

6.2 When you find what look like useful websites, complete the tables on the next page.

Topic	Urbanisation
Title of article	
Authority (who wrote it)	
Date (currency)	
Contents (a brief summary)	
Accuracy	
Audience	

Topic	Sustainable Development
Title of article	
Authority (who wrote it)	
Date (currency)	
Contents (a brief summary)	
Accuracy	
Audience	

Task 7: Acknowledging your sources

7.1 Why do you think it is important to reference the sources you use when writing a project? Add your ideas to the box below.

> **Reasons for reference sources:**
>
> **1** _To show where your ideas originated from – acknowledging the source._
>
> **2** _____
>
> **3** _____
>
> **4** _____

7.2 Compare your ideas with the information below. Whenever you use information from other sources, there are certain conventions you need to follow. There are two different aspects to acknowledging a source:

- **within your essay**, refer to the author by surname and the date of publication (textual reference);
- list your reference **at the end of your essay**, giving detailed information of the source (bibliography or references).

Reasons for referencing a source

- To show where your idea originated from – acknowledge the source.
- To show that you have done research to find 'evidence' for your viewpoint; references help to give your text academic 'weight'.
- To show that you are aware of the opinions/views expressed by writers in the field.
- To allow the reader to look at the original source if necessary.

Not referencing your sources, and thus failing to acknowledge other peoples' ideas, is considered to be plagiarism. This is not accepted academically. You will learn more about this in Unit 4.

> **Ways of referring to a source**
>
> - **Quotation:** Citing the exact words of the author
> - **Paraphrasing:** Retelling what the writer said, in your own words.
> - **Summarising:** Identifying the point you want to make from your source, and writing it in your own words. Whereas a paraphrase will include all the detail, a summary will be shorter, and will include only the key information.

Generally, writers use a mixture of summarising and paraphrasing, and only use quotations occasionally. Usually, quotations should only be used 'when you feel that the author expresses an idea or opinion in such a way that it is impossible to improve upon it or when you feel that it captures an idea in a particularly succinct and interesting way' (Trzeciak and Mackay, 1994).

Academic conventions in referencing

With direct quotations you can indent the quote, or put it in quotation marks. See the examples below. The quotation is usually written in a smaller font. In both cases you must include the page number.

A quotation of more than two lines

There are a number of views about what constitutes successful verbal communication. One area to consider is the people involved in a conversation, but as suggested below there are cultural restrictions on coming to a conclusion about this:

> A good conversation partner tends to empathise with others, being sufficiently aware to jointly create a conversation; this contrasts with American discourse patterns where conversations seem to be displays of antagonism (Lo Castro, 1987:105).

First of all, we need to consider what it is meant by 'to empathise with others' in Lo Castro's context.

A quotation of two lines or less

There are a number of views about what constitutes successful verbal communication. One area to consider is the people involved in a conversation, but there are cultural restrictions on coming to a conclusion about this:

> A good conversation partner tends to empathise with others, being sufficiently aware to jointly create a conversation (Lo Castro, 1987:105).

First of all, we need to consider what is meant by 'to empathise with others' in Lo Castro's context.

A quotation within a quotation

As stated by Adams (1999):

> 'internationally, the dominant definition of sustainable development has undoubtedly been that of the Brundtland Report: "development that meets the needs of the present without compromising the ability of future generations to meet their own needs" (Brundtland, 1987:45)'.

If you are paraphrasing or summarising, you can:

a) summarise or paraphrase the writer's ideas and put the author's surname and date of publication in brackets at the end of the sentence:

> **Since the cultural values of any society have an effect on how the people of that culture interact, sociocultural norms determine linguistic production, as well as limit how it is produced (Gumperz, 1983).**

b) refer directly to the author in the text and put the publication date in brackets:

> **According to Gumperz (1989), since the cultural values of any society have an effect on how the people of that culture interact, sociocultural norms determine linguistic production, as well as limit how it is produced.**

c) refer to the author directly and put his/her surname and the publication date in brackets at the end of the sentence:

> **According to Cottrell, there are seven approaches to learning which can make it more productive (Cottrell, 1999).**

Internet sources

As with printed sources, when referencing an Internet source within a text you need the author's surname and date. In this case, the date is when the website was last updated. In some cases the information may have been put up by an organisation, with no single author's name. In this case you include the name of the organisation within your written text, i.e. organisation and date. You do not include the website address in your main text; this goes in the bibliography.

> **The UK Government view on the use of natural resources is that it is possible to continue using them, but at the same time the development of alternative sources such as renewable energy should be considered (UK Government, 2003).**

Task 8: When not to use a website

Look at the statement below:

If you cannot find either an author or the name of an organisation on the website, you should not use it in your work. You should also check when the source was most recently updated.

Why do you think this is good advice? List some reasons below:

_____

_____

_____

_____

_____

_____

_____

Task 9: Writing a bibliography

9.1 Look at the bibliographical entry below. Match the labels a) to j) with the elements of a bibliographical entry 1–10 in the box below.

a) Title of article _____

b) Name of publisher _____

c) Date of publication _____

d) Author's surname _____

e) Title of book _____

f) Editor's name _____

g) Place of publication _____

h) Author's initials _____

i) Other editors _____

j) Shows book is a collection _____ of articles or chapters

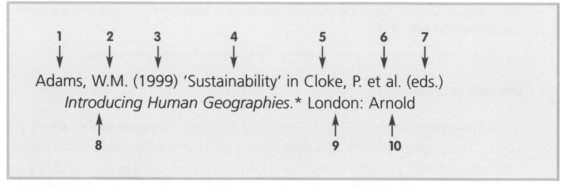

* It is the title of the book or journal, which goes in italics, not the title of the chapter or article.

Now look at the rest of the bibliography, which has been set out appropriately.

> Anderson, A.J. 2/02/2002 *Going Where the Big Guys Don't Go* http://www.businessweek.com viewed 03/09/02
>
> Cottrell, S. (1999) *The Study Skills Handbook*. London: Macmillan Press Ltd.
>
> Leki, U. and Carson, J. (1997) 'Completely different words: EAP and the writing experiences of ESL students in university courses' *TESOL Quarterly* 30/2: 201–204

9.2 There are some problems with the bibliography on page 39. Identify the problems and rewrite the bibliography in the appropriate form. Use the sample bibliography and the guide in Appendix 5 to help you.

9.3 Check your answers in small groups

Alan Bilham-Boult et al. 1999. People, Places and Themes. Heinemann, pp. 17-22

Adams, W.M. 1999. Sustainability. In P. Cloke et al. (eds) *Introducing Human Geographies*. Arnold, pp 125-129

'Africa Recovery' E. Harch (2003). {online}. Available from: http://www.africarecovery.org Accessed 18 May 2004

P. Newman, Transport: reducing automobile dependence. In D. Satterwaite (ed.) *The Earthscan Reader in Sustainable Cities*. Earthscan Publications pp 67-92 (1999)

For further practice on writing bibliographies, do the exercises at **http://www.englishforacademicstudy.com**.

4 Developing your project

In this unit you will:
- find out how to make the best use of the tutorial system;
- learn about plagiarism and how to avoid it;
- learn about the features of abstracts and their purpose.

The tutorial system

A tutorial is a private meeting between your teacher (who may be called your personal tutor) and you (the tutee). Your tutor will probably have several tutees. Usually, you will meet with your tutor to discuss academic issues. If you have other problems such as accommodation problems, ill health or concerns about your future studies, then you may be expected to speak to someone else, possibly a non-academic member of staff. You might want to check with your tutor whether this is the best course of action, but it is not usually the tutor's role to advise you about non-academic matters.

The appointment system

Usually, your tutor will arrange an appointment schedule for you and the other tutees. Often, tutors post appointment times on the classroom wall and/or door. Your tutor may set up a system for notifying you of appointments by e-mail or through the use of Blackboard or a similar virtual learning environment. Your tutor may decide when and how often you should attend a tutorial, or he/she may simply leave a blank form for you to fill in your preferred time. See below:

The appointment (sample)

Date	Time	Name
August 15th	2.15	Suzy
August 15th	2.35	Ali
August 16th	2.15	Cai

Making the best use of tutorial time

Tutorials may last anything from a few minutes to more than half an hour; usually, you will have a specific time allocated, e.g. 20 minutes. For this reason, it is important to come to tutorials well-prepared. It is your responsibility to get the most you can from the tutorial in the short time that you have. Therefore, you should think about the questions you want to ask before you attend a tutorial, e.g. aspects of your project you want to discuss or any questions about your feedback or classwork which need clarification. You should know exactly what information you want to find out about before you have your tutorial. You should also bring a notebook so that you can make a brief note of any information or advice you get. However, you will not have time to write down everything during the tutorial – just headings. Therefore, you should make notes immediately after the tutorial while the information related to your discussion is still fresh in your head.

You may find that some tutors on your academic course are less patient and understanding than many of the teachers on a pre-sessional course, which makes preparation for tutorials all the more important.

Task 1: Preparing for tutorials

Imagine that you have just received the feedback sheet below from your project teacher after completing the first draft of a project.

Read through the feedback sheet and then prepare a set of questions you would like information or advice about during a 20-minute tutorial.

To what extent can the problems of urban development be met by a policy of sustainable development?

Content	You have lots of information here, but it is still very descriptive. Think about what you have been reading – what is your opinion about it?
Organisation	Try to link the introduction and conclusion to the main body of the text.
Language	Check the grammatical use of 'according to'. Check how to use the present perfect tense.
Presentation of work	Make sure you have used the correct font size for headings. You have not used the appropriate style in the main body of your text.
Use of sources	You use sources on the first page – but then not any more. Any idea that comes from a source you have used must be referenced. What happened to your list of references at the end?

Avoiding plagiarism

You are now familiar with referencing and why it is important in academic writing.

Sometimes when you are summarising ideas, even if the source is acknowledged, the ideas you express may be too similar to the original. You need to use your own words as far as possible to avoid this. Obviously, there may be certain specialist words or key words in the original text that you need to use in order to explain concepts or ideas. But it is important to avoid writing something that is too close to the original – even if you think the writer can express the ideas much better than you can. Read the text with your purpose clearly in your mind.

a) Take notes of the information you might use.

b) Organise your ideas about the information and, if possible, explain them to someone else.
If you cannot explain the text you have read clearly, you may not have fully understood it.

c) Write up the information you need for your project based on your notes.

Remember the **N.O.W.** approach from Unit 2 (page 18).

What is plagiarism?

The word plagiarism derives from a Latin word meaning *thief*. Plagiarism is a form of academic theft. In its most blatant form it involves word-for-word copying of large sections of another writer's material and claiming it as your own work. In a less extreme, but no less acceptable form, it involves reproducing shorter lines or phrases linked together, perhaps with minor modifications, in the pretence that these are your ideas expressed in your own words.

Therefore, it is essential to express your ideas appropriately and acknowledge your sources. If you do not do this, it is the equivalent of stealing ideas. Look at the University of Reading's policy on this below. The complete information is on the university website. There are also some guidelines on how you can avoid plagiarism. The statement made in the box below is an extract from the University of Reading website section titled ACADEMIC MISCONDUCT:

ACADEMIC MISCONDUCT

Statement on cheating

The University's statement on academic misconduct is as follows:

Cheating, which is an attempt to gain an advantage for oneself or another by deceit, and other misconduct are breaches of discipline under the University's Regulations for Conduct 32(b), and are punishable by a range of sanctions.

a) Cheating in assessed coursework (for example, dissertations, long essays or projects) and open book examinations includes:

Plagiarism: the misrepresentation of the work of others as one's own (including ideas, arguments, words, diagrams, images or data). It includes the explicit claim that another's work is one's own and, no less seriously, the failure to acknowledge adequately the sources used. This applies whatever the source of the material (for example, a published source, the World-Wide Web, a verbal communication, or the work of another student). Plagiarism is a form of academic misconduct and will be penalised accordingly.

b) Cheating and other academic misconduct in written examinations includes:

Plagiarism: while it is recognised that in a written examination ideas, arguments and phrases may not be as fully or as precisely acknowledged as in coursework, the deliberate substantial reproduction of another's work in a written examination without acknowledgement is an offence.

Source: *http://www.rdg.ac.uk/Exams/staff/misconduct.htm* Viewed 28 October, 2004

As you can see, you must never plagiarise. The consequences could be serious and could damage your academic career and indeed your chances of getting a job.

Task 2: Quotations, paraphrases and plagiarism

Imagine a student has highlighted the following extract in a politics textbook.

> Gorbachev declared that the countries of the world shared mutual interests and faced mutual threats that went beyond class conflict. This was a revolutionary perspective for a Soviet leader, because a Marxist-Leninist class conflict was the ultimate driving force behind history (Papp, 1994: 290).

The student has decided to use ideas from this extract in an essay. There are a number of ways he/she could do this. Consider the following possibilities (1–7 below).

2.1   Decide whether the incorporation is either a quote or a paraphrase and place a tick (✓) in the appropriate column.

2.2   Decide whether you think the student would be guilty of plagiarism and place a tick (✓) in the appropriate column.

Incorporated text	Quote	Paraphrase	Plagiarism
1 But by this time things were changing in Russia. The new leader, Gorbachev, argued that all countries in the world had interests in common, which were not connected with class. This was very different from the traditional Soviet view. (Papp, 1994: 290)			
2 But by this time things were changing in Russia. Gorbachev declared that the countries of the world shared mutual interests and faced mutual threats that went beyond class conflict. This was a revolutionary perspective for a Soviet leader, because a Marxist-Leninist class conflict was the ultimate driving force behind history. The West reacted to this new way of talking …			
3 But by now things were changing in Russia, where the new leader was talking about how the different countries of the world faced similar problems. Such beliefs represented a complete break with standard Soviet philosophy. The West reacted to the new mood in the USSR by …			
4 But by now things were changing in Russia. Established Soviet dogma was being abandoned by the new leader, whose views concerning the common interests of different countries in the world, both East and West, clearly represented a revolutionary perspective for a leader of the USSR. The West reacted to such changes by …			

Incorporated text	Quote	Paraphrase	Plagiarism
5 But by now things were changing in Russia. The new leader was expressing views which were very different from traditional Soviet ideology. As one theorist puts it: Gorbachev declared that the countries of the world shared mutual interests and faced mutual threats that went beyond class conflict. This was a revolutionary perspective for a Soviet leader, because a Marxist-Leninist class conflict was the ultimate driving force behind history (Papp, 1994: 290).			
6 But by now things were changing in Russia. The new leader was expressing views that were very different from traditional Soviet ideology, in that they represented a revolutionary perspective for a leader of the USSR in which the class struggle was the driving force. The West reacted to such changes …			
7 But by now things were changing in Russia. The new leader was expressing views about the need for international action that were so different from established Soviet ideology that they represented a "revolutionary perspective for a Soviet leader" (Papp, 1994: 290). The West reacted to the new Soviet mood by …			

Source: Papp, D.S. (1994) Contemporary International Relations: frameworks for understanding. New York Macmillan.

Task 3: Avoiding plagiarism

Here are some reasons that students might give for plagiarising. What advice would you give them?

a) I didn't know it was wrong.

Your advice: _____

_____

_____

_____

_____

b) I didn't know how to use references.

Your advice: _____

_____

_____

_____

_____

c) I didn't have enough time to do the necessary reading, or to develop my own ideas.

Your advice: _____

_____

_____

_____

d) The text was so difficult for me to understand that I just copied the text and hoped it was OK.

Your advice: _____

_____

_____

_____

e) The text I copied said exactly what I wanted to say and I couldn't express it better.

Your advice: _____

_____

_____

_____

f) In my country, we are expected to reproduce the exact words and ideas of the text or the teacher.

Your advice: _____

_____

_____

_____

Working with abstracts

An abstract is a form of summary. It can be used to summarise the contents of an academic text, such as an academic paper, a journal article or an oral presentation. It is very useful to look at abstracts in order to quickly find out about the main ideas of a text, and thus whether the text is relevant to your needs. Often, when carrying out research, you will initially find many sources that appear to be relevant, and it is difficult to decide which sources to concentrate on. However, by referring to abstracts first, you will be able to decide more quickly and make informed decisions.

Students are expected to include abstracts at the beginning of pieces of extended writing, as well as submitting an abstract if they are going to give an oral presentation based on their project.

As with introductions and conclusions, abstracts have certain typical features.

Task 4: Features of abstracts

4.1 Read abstracts A and B. What features can you identify?

For example:
Essential background information

ABSTRACT A

In-company Business English training takes place within the competitive commercial field. Clients demand the same levels of quality and effectiveness from a course provider that they expect in all commercial enterprises. In order to meet the expected standards, the product and the service have to be good. Therefore, to demonstrate a commitment to quality and good service, and to be successful in this competitive market, course providers must invest time and resources in training for Business English teachers. The success of a Business English course is largely in the hands of the teacher. This investigation looks into teachers' attitudes to and perceptions of Business English teaching to see whether they have the level of confidence, experience and knowledge needed to perform effectively in the field. The results of analysing these perceptions, along with the training needs that are identified, will be incorporated into future in-service training provision for Business English teachers.

ABSTRACT B

Assessment of observed teaching practice sessions on teacher training courses is viewed in general by the teaching profession as a flawed but necessary method of evaluation. The nature of observations means that criteria must be flexible to account for diverse teaching styles, while at the same time providing the observer with the guidance to make an informed decision on the trainee's performance. Inevitably, observers have their own set of personal theories that affect their assessment, resulting in inconsistency of grades awarded by different observers.

The results suggest that standardisation can help effect greater observer agreement, but the limitations of the study mean that the results need ratification through further research. It was found that discussion of grades raised issues such as the need for clearer criteria for grades, the need to limit the list of attributes

4.2 Compare your ideas with the list of features below and tick (✓) the features you have identified.

a) a general statement ☐

b) essential background information ☐

c) the aims of the project, dissertation or thesis ☐

d) an investigation into a particular topic or subject area ☐

e) the implementation of the investigation in a real-world situation ☐

f) how the text is organised ☐

g) details of the research carried out by the writer ☐

h) what the results of the research suggest ☐

i) a thesis statement ☐

j) a definition ☐

4.3 Look at abstracts C and D. Do these two abstracts have the same features as abstracts A and B? What other features of abstracts do they contain? (Refer to the list above.)

ABSTRACT C

This project describes the development of China's securities market while analysing its shortcomings. It also discusses some recently proposed solutions. During the last ten years, significant progress has been made in a very short time in terms of the market scale and trading facilities, even by Western standards. This project describes the main achievements in China's securities market. However, this market has not achieved full credibility due to problems, such as an inefficient regulatory framework, high speculation, corporate governance deficiency and undue government intervention. To deal with these problems, several methods are being considered, which include the government changing the labour laws, the introduction of new initiatives, and the strengthening of self-regulation in the supervision process. The government will also ensure that this legislation is enforced.

ABSTRACT D

Banking has developed over the last 300 years. Due to advances in technology, banks can provide a variety of products for their customers. In 1947, banks began to issue credit cards. In the last 20 years, they have become their most advanced financial product. In Taiwan, major development of credit cards began in 1983. However, only three banks are making a profit in the credit card market. It is very important, therefore, for Taiwanese banking to develop an understanding of the credit card system used in the West. This paper will begin with an introduction to the credit card business, and then describe early developments in the industry in certain Western countries. Secondly, the recent developments in the Taiwanese credit card market are addressed. Finally, the extent to which Taiwanese banks should absorb Western practices in promoting their credit card business is discussed.

Now read Abstract E.

ABSTRACT E

With the steady development of economic globalisation, risk has become a controversial issue for financial institutions and non-financial firms. The management goals for banking or individual firms are no longer simply to gain profits but to try to control risk in order to gain maximum profits. This project aims to discuss the important role of managing risk and show the most effective way to manage it. Firstly, a definition of risk is provided, as well as a classification of the forms of risk. The project then goes on to discuss the different financial instruments used to manage risk, followed by an evaluation of the economic effect of risk management for financial institutions. It concludes by suggesting that risk cannot be fully avoided because the world is always changing and so is the financial environment.

4.4 Each of the above abstracts (A–E) refers to a project written by a former pre-sessional student. Based on your reading of each abstract, suggest what you think the titles of the projects were. The title for Abstract A is given as an example.

Abstract	Possible title
A	Teachers' attitudes to and perceptions of Business English teaching
B	
C	
D	
E	

5 Developing a focus

In this unit you will:
- learn how to choose a topic;
- practise narrowing down the topic to establish a focus;
- come up with a working title.

One of the most challenging aspects of working on a project is establishing a title and deciding exactly what you will work on. It needs to be a topic that you can narrow down enough to establish a clear focus, so that the project is not too general. This is not always easy to do, as you may be interested in many aspects of a topic. However, isolating one particular aspect allows you to explore a subject in more depth, which is what is required in your academic work.

STEPS IN GETTING STARTED

You will have encountered the following stages in Unit 1 Task 4:

- Choosing a topic

- Brainstorming ideas

- Narrowing the focus by asking yourself questions

- Establishing a working title which is flexible and developmental

- Choosing some of your sources by looking at journals, books and websites

Task 1: Choosing a topic for your extended essay

Choosing a topic for your extended essay requires careful consideration and organisation. If you choose a topic that is too specialised, you may find it difficult to find suitable sources of information. However, if you choose a topic that is too general, you may find there is too much information available, thus making it difficult for you to decide which information to use.

Because you are working in your own subject area, you need to display a level of specialised knowledge that shows you have a deeper understanding of the subject. At the same time, you need to consider who your reader is. Any piece of work you produce should be accessible to the average interested reader; in other words, the reader should not need to be an expert in the field.

Below are some steps in the process of choosing a topic, but they are not in the correct order. Put them in the correct order by numbering the list 1–8, as appropriate.

a) Decide how practical it is to work on this topic.

b) Find something in your subject area you are interested in.

c) Summarise your project idea in one sentence.

d) Decide how much you already know about the topic. ☐

e) Talk about your ideas. ☐

f) Think about a possible working title. ☐

g) Look for sources. ☐

h) Make a plan. ☐

Task 2: Developing a topic – Global warming

Look at the following essay titles and put each in one of the three columns below, according to how general or specific it is.

a) Bangladesh under water: what made it happen?

b) How to combat climate change

c) Three results of global warming on China

d) Increased rainfall: a sign of future weather

e) The causes and effects of global warming

f) The melting poles: the greatest danger from climate change

g) What is global warming?

h) The economic effects of climate change

i) The effect of temperature increases on maize production

Most general ➡	⬅ General ➡ ⬅ Specific ➡	⬅ Most specific

Task 3: Establishing a focus

There are three stages in producing a project: planning, researching and writing up. In each of these stages there are a number of smaller steps.

One way to establish a focus for your topic is to ask yourself questions about the topic. For example, 'Tourism' is a very general topic. In order to get specific ideas about this topic, you could ask yourself some specific WH– questions. WH– questions are: *Why? Who? What? Where? When? Which? How?* You may not always ask all these questions.

For example:
Why is tourism important?
Who is affected by tourism?
What is tourism?
Where does tourism have most impact?
Which countries are most dependent on tourism?
How is tourism affecting native culture?

3.1 Now make a list of your own questions for the following topic, based on the example above:

The Education System in Argentina

3.2 Here are some general subjects chosen by students. How could they be changed, using some of the questions above, so that each topic is more specific or focused?

- Problems in the Chinese economy
- The economy of Taiwan
- Cybernetics
- The United Nations
- Genetically modified (GM) food
- Deforestation in Nepal
- Future developments in human health

Task 4: Establishing a working title

A working title is a title that you initially think of in order to establish a focus for your research and writing. As you read and become more involved in the subject of your project, your viewpoint may change. This is all part of the process of developing your ideas, and thus part of fine-tuning your research skills. You may decide to go back and change your plan, and your final title may differ somewhat from your working title.

Look at the following example of a working title below, created by a pre-sessional student, below. This student felt that the original working title was too general. The student experimented with a second working title before arriving at the third and final title.

> **Pollution and its relationship with people and the environment**

> **The social and environmental impact of pollution**

> **The environmental impact of pollution in urban areas**

4.1 Look at the titles below. Some of them lack focus. Rewrite those that you think could be improved by making them more specific.

a) Economics affects everything we do.

_____

_____

_____

b) The origin of genetic engineering.

_____

_____

_____

c) The effect of electronics on society.

_____

_____

_____

4.2 Now choose two topics, related to your subject area, and develop your own working titles, going through the stages above. You do not need to write projects on these titles, but the task gives you practice in focusing on specific areas and helps you to be more precise when you write.

_____

_____

_____

_____

_____

_____

_____

_____

_____

Task 5: Planning your project

You will already have done some reading, research and thinking about your project. Based on this, fill in the table as far as possible.

What is your topic?

_____

_____

Why have you chosen this topic?

_____

_____

_____

_____

_____

Key questions (What do you want to find out about this topic?)

_____

_____

_____

_____

_____

_____

What is your focus and/or working title?

Thesis statement

Specific title*

* This may develop later, or you may not know this until you have carried out some research in the library or on-line.

6 Introductions, conclusions and definitions

In this unit you will:
- analyse the features of introductions;
- analyse the features of conclusions;
- analyse the features of definitions;
- identify the language of each of these components in a typical academic text.

Introductions

While writing an academic text such as a project, it is important to think about the structure and to focus on individual components of the text.

The introduction is important as the first part of your essay; it sets the tone for the reader, gives some idea of the content and the writer's position, and suggests how the piece of work is organised. In Unit 1, you brainstormed ideas on what to include in an introduction. For Task 5 (page 11), you developed definitions for sustainable development and urbanisation, you introduced some background information on the problems of urbanisation and policies of sustainable development, and you also developed a thesis statement. These are some of the key features that can be included in an introduction.

Below is a more complete list of such features:

a) Introduction to the topic of your essay

b) Background information about your topic

c) Justification for your choice of topic focus

d) Outline of the structure of the essay

e) Definition of key terms related to the topic

f) Thesis statement (your viewpoint or perspective)

g) Your purpose in writing the essay

Pre-task activity

There are four introductions below. Each one contains some of the features (a–g) outlined above. Certain features have been identified in the first introduction, as an example.

First, discuss the features of Introduction 1 with a partner and then look at how certain features can be identified (Table 1).

THE APPLICATION OF RENEWABLE ENERGY TECHNOLOGY IN REMOTE AREAS

Our life is heavily dependent on the supply of energy. After World War II, especially, developed countries received the great benefits of electricity. However, today more than 30% of the global population still live in off-grid areas, without electricity. This is mostly in developing countries or remote parts of developed countries, such as mountainous areas or isolated islands. Economically, it would be very challenging to produce electricity for these areas. As developing countries grow economically, the demand for energy will increase rapidly, thus adding to the pollution problems caused by fossil fuels. Renewable energy technology is the solution to these problems. This essay will first demonstrate the need for electricity in remote areas, and then the extent to which renewable energy technology can meet this need in remote areas will be examined by looking at some examples.

Table 1: Features of Introduction 1

Feature	Example from text
Introduction to topic	Our life is heavily dependent on the supply of energy.
Background information	After World War II, especially, developed countries received the great benefits of electricity. However, today more than 30% of the global population still live in off-grid areas, without electricity. This is mostly in developing countries or remote parts of developed countries, such as mountainous areas or isolated islands.
Justification	To show the problems related to the production of electricity in developing countries, as well as the pollution caused by using fossil fuels.
Outline of structure	This essay will first demonstrate the demand for electricity in remote areas, and then the extent to which renewable energy technology can meet this need in remote areas will be examined by looking at some examples.
Definition of key terms	Not included.
Thesis statement	Renewable energy technology is the solution to these problems.
Writer's purpose	To show how to overcome the problem (by using renewable energy technology).

From your discussion about the introduction, it will be clear that certain features overlap, e.g., background information may be considered in part as justification, and the thesis statement may be linked with the writer's purpose. Furthermore, certain features are not always included, for example, in this introduction there is no definition of *renewable energy*.

Task 1: Features of introductions

1.1 Identify the features listed above in each of Introductions 2–4. Underline these features and write the letter (a–g) in the margin opposite each feature.

1.2 Discuss your analysis of the introductions in small groups. Complete the summary table on page 58 by ticking (✓) the appropriate columns.

Introduction 2

BRAND COMMUNICATION IN CHINA

Since China began to develop economically and to open up to world trade in the early 1980s, many international companies have entered the Chinese market. In the beginning, many worldwide companies entered the market with confidence and kept their customary management system and market strategy approach. However, they soon found this approach was not suitable for the Chinese economic environment, and they had to find a way to adapt to the new situation. Some of the European and American companies cooperated with Japanese companies, because they wanted to utilise the Japanese experience in the Asian market when marketing their products. They were interested in brand communication, which involves using a series of effective marketing strategies. This approach appears to work well in China. The issue of brand communication, including examining why this approach is necessary, and the steps involved in setting up promotion techniques to promote the prestige of a brand, will be discussed in this project.

Introduction 3

DOWNSIZING AS A NECESSITY FOR SURVIVAL

Over the past decade, an uncertain economic climate and the rapid development of technology have led to an increasingly sophisticated business environment. Under these rapid changes, in order to gain competitive advantages, organisations are being increasingly reoriented or converged. Downsizing (Steven et al., 1998) is a response to the external environment, as companies are attempting to reposition themselves so as to gain a competitive advantage in an uncertain marketplace. Emphasis is on 'lean and mean' as an effective way for organisations to achieve the 'lean' purposes of downsizing. Downsizing is necessary for survival in many cases. If human resource managers lack an appropriate downsizing programme, they will be faced with negative feedback from employees. As a result, it will lead to the opposite effect to the 'lean' performance and efficient purposes of downsizing. This project will examine how to present a positive vision of downsizing to employees. First, the purpose of downsizing will be addressed. Then, examples of the characteristics of an effective downsizing process will be examined. In the final part, three sets of data that evaluate the process of downsizing will be explored.

THE DEVELOPMENT OF A GLOBAL COMPANY

'Global' means worldwide. But how does a company become a global company? Are there benefits to becoming a global company? This essay will first explain what a global company is, and then look at the difference between this and a non-global company. Secondly, the essay will explain global strategy and the benefits of global strategies. Finally, a case study of the globalising development of Philips will be considered.

Summary table

Feature	Introduction 2	Introduction 3	Introduction 4
Introduction to topic			
Background information			
Justification			
Outline of structure			
Definition of key terms			
Thesis statement			
Writer's purpose			

Task 2: Analysing your introduction

2.1 Look at the introduction for your own project. Which of the above features can you identify? Place a tick (✓) in the appropriate row of the table below.

Feature	My project	My partner's project
Introduction to topic		
Background information		
Justification		
Outline of structure		
Definition of key terms		
Thesis statement		
Writer's purpose		

2.2 Exchange your introduction with a partner – which features can you identify in their work?

2.3 Now compare your findings. Are there any other features you found that are not on the list? You may need to discuss this with your teacher.

Task 3: The language of introductions

Look again at Introductions 1–4.

Underline any expressions or phrases in these introductions that you think might be useful. You may be able to use some of these in your own academic writing.

For example:

Introduction 1: This essay will first demonstrate ... and then ... will be examined by looking at some examples.

Conclusions

The conclusion at the end of your essay serves a number of functions. It is the final part of your text and so needs to pull together all the main ideas. It should refer back to what you outlined in your introduction and to your thesis. It is an opportunity to show the extent to which you have been able to deal with the issues involved in your thesis. Conclusions may have some or all of the following features:

a) A logical conclusion that is evident from the development of the ideas in your essay

b) A brief summary of the main ideas in the essay

c) Comments on these ideas

d) Predictions for future developments of the topic

e) Mention of further research that might be required

f) Limitations of the work covered by your essay

Task 4: Features of conclusions

Look at Conclusions 1–4 (pages 60 and 61), all of which contain some of the features outlined above.

4.1 Identify the features from the list above in each of the conclusions. Underline the features and write the letter (a–f) in the margin opposite the feature in the text.

4.2 Discuss your analysis of the conclusions in small groups.

4.3 Complete the table on page 61 by ticking (✓) the appropriate columns.

Conclusion 1

THE IMPACT OF TECHNOLOGY TRANSFER BY MULTINATIONAL CORPORATIONS

Whereas the aim of this essay was to evaluate the effect of technology transfer brought about by multinational corporations (MNCs), it has become a kind of summary of some researchers' theories. However, certain conclusions can be drawn.

Although investment into less developed countries by multinational corporations has many positive effects, there are also some problems. One of these is the problem of employee training. As mentioned in Section 3, with the present state of affairs, technology diffusion into developing countries via vocational training is not working effectively. One possible reason is that MNCs have to protect their advantage of knowledge and investment-intensive technology in order not to lose their competitiveness in the market. The reason MNCs invest in less developed countries is to achieve the comparative advantage of low wages and cheap resources. Although vocational training is essential for multinational corporations to succeed in the markets of these countries, they do not directly aim to develop the level of technology in less developed countries. In other words, the progress of technology in less developed countries is the secondary product of multinational enterprises. The original idea that this technology would transfer beyond efficient employee training for a specific purpose seems to have been an idealistic theoretical concept. However, if this situation is not changed, the technological gap between developed countries and developing countries will increase, leading to a widening of the gap between rich developed countries and poor developing countries.

Fortunately, as mentioned in Section 4, sophisticated companies have begun to realise their social responsibility, and recently have been trying to cooperate with governments and non-governmental organisations. It is to be hoped that this trend will continue, and thus MNCs will make a contribution to less developed countries through the development of transferable skills that can be applied to technological development, rather than using less developed countries purely for their own benefit.

Conclusion 2

THE APPLICATION OF RENEWABLE ENERGY TECHNOLOGY IN REMOTE AREAS

Industrialised countries have received a considerable number of benefits from energy, especially electricity, and the demand for energy has been increasing. However, as discussed above, there are still many people who do not have access to electric light, as a conventional energy supply system is not suitable in remote areas. In order to solve the energy crisis in remote areas, renewable energy technology has great potential. Although only two kinds of technologies have been examined in this work, other renewable energy technologies are advantageous, and these technologies have also been accepted in some areas as a main energy supply system. Nevertheless, even if renewable energy technologies are applied, it is not easy to establish the technology in poor societies. When this technology is applied, the concept of appropriate technology is extremely important. The designer needs to grasp the economic, technical, social and cultural background of the area. He/she also needs to think of the characteristics of each technology, as well as climatic conditions. Only well-planned appropriate technology that takes these factors into consideration will work in solving the serious energy problems in remote areas.

Conclusion 3

LANGUAGE APTITUDE AS A FACTOR IN SECOND LANGUAGE LEARNING

This essay has discussed the features of language aptitude. It has emerged that language aptitude is often applied to the classroom situation, but not in real-life situations. As second language acquisition is such a complicated process, it is necessary to explore the influence of age, motivation, attitude, personality and the mother tongue, in order to understand the process more fully. It would be interesting to examine how these factors can influence language learning, and compensate for the natural aptitude that learners possess to a greater or lesser extent, as this project has shown.

Conclusion 4

WHY WAS THE RESTRUCTURING OF THE KOREAN BANKING SYSTEM SUCCESSFUL?

In the spate of bank crises in Asia, Korea's banking system also suffered the hardest time in its history. Seventeen commercial banks were closed and more than 40,000 bank employees were expelled from their companies. It cost 137.1 trillion won (equivalent to 110 billion US dollars) to restore the banking system. The crisis was inevitable because it was an eruption of deep-rooted problems, such as policy mistakes and poor bank management. However, Korea's banks successfully weathered the crisis. As of June 2002, Korea's banks recorded an historically high net profit, and their capital structures are the soundest in the world. Future prospects are good.

There are a number of factors which contributed to this success. Of these success factors, the following seem to be key. First, the Korean government followed many valuable lessons suggested by empirical studies. For example, it set up prompt and massive action plans, including a huge amount of public funds. It also maintained its strict stances at all times. It introduced a considerable number of standard global regulations and incentive systems to enhance the competition. Secondly, change in the political power of the time played a key role in implementing strict policies for restructuring. As the new government was relatively free from responsibility for the crisis and political interests, they could undertake firm action. Thirdly, nationwide consensus for changes strongly supported government reforms. The Korean people knew that change was needed in order to survive. Eventually, encouraged by nationwide consensus, the new government dared to challenge the tough task of restructuring the banking system.

Summary table

Feature	Conclusion 1	Conclusion 2	Conclusion 3	Conclusion 4
Logical conclusion				
Brief summary				
Comments on ideas				
Predictions				
Further research				
Limitations				

Task 5: Analysing your conclusion

5.1 Look at the conclusion of your own project. Which of the features (a–f) on page 59 can you identify? Place a tick (✓) in the appropriate row of the table below.

Feature	My project	My partner's project
Logical conclusion		
Brief summary		
Comments on ideas		
Predictions		
Further research		
Limitations		

5.2 Exchange your conclusion with a partner – which features can you identify in their work?

5.3 Now compare your findings. Are there any other features you found that are not on the list? You may need to discuss this with your teacher.

Task 6: The language of conclusions

Look again at the Conclusions 1–4.

Underline any expressions or phrases you think might be useful in your own academic writing.

For example:

Conclusion 1: Whereas the aim of this essay was to evaluate ... it has become a summary of some researchers' theories.

Extended definitions

When writing about a topic, it is essential that you clarify your terms, i.e., explain clearly what is meant by key words that you use. If you were writing about Human Resource Management, for example, you would need to explain what you mean by Human Resources, so that both the writer and reader have exactly the same interpretation of the term. You will often find that definitions form at least part of introductory texts to your subject area. The extent to which you need to define your terms will depend on your reader and your purpose for writing. For example, if you are new to the subject area, then for yourself (as well, perhaps, for your tutor), you need to clarify some of the most basic terms. As you gain a deeper knowledge and understanding of the subject, and are writing for experts, the meaning of certain key terms can be assumed, as part of 'shared knowledge'.

Look at the example of a definition below.

Term	Definition
Academic Studies	*Academic Studies is a course that is designed to help students develop some of the research skills required in their future field of study.*

This definition in itself does not give you very much information about the course; an extended definition would be more useful. You might add to the short definition above in the following way, which explains what students are expected to do.

Term	Extended definition
Academic Studies	*Students work to produce an extended piece of writing on a topic in their subject area, and will also give an oral presentation on this topic. They are expected to read widely and select appropriate sources to support the ideas related to their topic. They work on summarising and synthesising information accurately, as well as evaluating what they read. They learn about the conventions of referencing and how to write a bibliography. They are expected to draw on the skills being developed in other components of the course, e.g., practising reading strategies by reading selectively, and working on the micro-skills of writing introductions and conclusions. The oral component of the course is also important, as students are expected to be able to discuss their ideas with both tutor and fellow students, as well as give a formal presentation. Students are to a large extent expected to work autonomously.*

Task 7: Features of definitions

Look at the four definitions below from the work of pre-sessional students.

7.1 Identify the features of the definitions (a–d) and complete the table on page 64 by ticking (✔) the appropriate cells.

    a) A formal definition, e.g. from a dictionary or expert in the field

    b) An expansion of the definition with an explanation and/or examples

    c) A comment on the definition by the writer

    d) References

7.2 Underline or annotate the relevant parts of the definitions and discuss them with a partner.

Feature	Definition 1	Definition 2	Definition 3	Definition 4
Formal definition				
Expansion				
Comment				
References				

Definition 1: Language Aptitude

Some people have a natural language ability, which makes them adept at learning foreign languages, whereas others are rather poor at it and struggle to acquire a basic communicative ability in the language. A factor which makes a difference to the individual is often referred to as language aptitude. Though difficult to define in concrete terms, it is understood to be not necessarily the ability to learn the language in the classroom, but rather to be able to apply this knowledge in a real-life situation (Cook 1991). While some people argue that this ability is not fixed, Carroll (1981) believes that aptitude is an innate or stable factor, which cannot be changed through training and is constant throughout one's life. He also insists that it is not related to past learning experience. This implies that language aptitude is not something that is accumulated as we age, but something we are born with. This may sound demotivating for those who are not equipped with language aptitude. However, as Ellis (1994) suggests, aptitude is only a facilitator which encourages learning, especially accelerating the rate of learning, but not determining learning.

Definition 2: Globalisation

The term 'globalisation' holds considerable interest. It refers to 'the increasing integration of economies around the world, particularly through trade and financial flows' (Oxford Advanced Learner Dictionary 2001). The term can also refer to the movement of people (labour) and knowledge (technology) across international borders. Globalisation can help countries get rid of the barriers to the inflow of technology, capital, human resources and products. Generally, globalisation makes the above more available, especially the accessibility of products. It can also speed up the development of foreign trade.

Definition 3: A Global Company

A global company can be defined as a corporation consisting of a group of people who run a business in different countries as one body (Uniglobe 2002). A global company is different from a non-global company. There are three main differences between a global company and a non-global company First of all, a global company should introduce its same-brand products worldwide at the same time. Secondly, a global company must inform its subsidiaries around the world of major management decisions. Thirdly, each subsidiary of the global company based in a different country must compete at a national level by taking local preferences into consideration.

Definition 4: Global

> The term 'global' (or 'transnational') implies the centralisation of management decision-making to overseas subsidiaries and highly efficient coordination of activities across national boundaries in pursuit of global competitiveness (Yip 1992; Bartlett and Ghoshol 1989). Geographically, global firms are similar to multinationals. Both are businesses operating in more than one country; however, they are totally different in nature. A multinational business refers to a company with branches in several countries with little coordination of activities, and decentralisation of management decision-making (Bartnett and Ghoshol 1989).

Task 8: Effective definitions

Discuss the following in small groups.

8.1 Which definition is the most useful for the reader?

8.2 Explain your choice.

Remember

- When you give a definition, it is essential not to write a circular definition, e.g. *an extended writing class is a class where students learn to write extended essays*. This is not a helpful definition for the reader who wants to understand the meaning of an *extended essay class*.

- It is recommended that an acknowledged source of reference is used, e.g. a dictionary or a recognised authority in the field. However, it is also important to comment on the definition, especially if you are looking at several sources with differing definitions. If you refer to more than one definition, it is important to clearly state which definition you prefer.

Task 9: Practice definition

Write an extended definition of your own subject area. Make sure that you include all of the features included in the definitions above. Your audience consists of your classmates and your teacher, who are not experts in the field, so remember to use terminology that you can easily explain.

_____

_____

_____

_____

_____

_____

_____

_____

_____

7 Incorporating data and illustrations

In this unit you will:
- learn how data is incorporated into academic texts;
- learn how to analyse data;
- practise using the language of data commentary.

Another aspect of academic writing is data commentary. Data is statistical information that may be presented graphically in the form of tables or figures. Data is used to support the information and ideas of the academic researcher. An illustration might be, for example, a photograph or diagram. In academic writing, illustrations should only be used to clarify ideas or information; in other words, they should enhance an explanation. If you include any data or illustrations in your academic texts, make sure that they have a purpose – they should not be used for decoration.

Task 1: The purpose of data

1.1 Answer the following questions from your own knowledge, or by using the information in this unit.

a) What is data?

_____

_____

_____

b) Why is data sometimes included in academic texts?

_____

_____

_____

c) Read the information on the next page, which comes from a text called *The facts about UK travel and tourism* (Youell, 1995).

- What is the purpose of Figure 1.21?
- What is the purpose of Figure 1.22?
- What main conclusion can you make from the data in Figure 1.22?
- What is the purpose of Table 1.5?
- What main conclusions can you draw from the data in Table 1.5?

1.2 Both of the figures and the table are accompanied by captions that briefly describe their content. What do you notice about these captions? Complete the following sentences.

a) The language style _____

_____

_____

b) The position of the caption _____

_____

_____

Text 7–1: The development of jet aircraft

The Development of Jet Aircraft

Fig. 1.21 A Boeing 767

The technological advances in aircraft design which resulted from developments during the Second World War led to air travel becoming a reality for the masses of the population from the 1950s onwards. The Boeing 707 jet was introduced in 1958 and led to a surge in scheduled and charter flights, the latter being combined with accommodation, transfers and courier services to form the 'package holiday' that is so familiar to us in the early twenty-first century (See Figure 1.21).

The Introduction of the Package Tour

The 1960s saw the beginning of the rapid increase in the number of package holidays sold. Destinations such as the coastal areas of Southern Spain, the Balearic Islands and Greece were favourite locations for British and other European travellers. The convenience of an all-inclusive arrangement, coupled with the increased speed which the new aircraft brought, caught the imagination of the British travelling public. The age of mass tourism had truly arrived.

Travel and Tourism Today

Tourism is now commonly referred to as 'the world's biggest industry'. According to the World Travel and Tourism Council (WTTC), in 1990 the industry:

- Generated an annual turnover equivalent to 5.9 per cent of the world GNP
- Employed 118 million people worldwide
- Accounted for over 6.7 per cent of the world's capital investment
- Contributed over 5.6 per cent to total tax payments worldwide

Figure 1.22 below shows the growth in travel and tourism gross output (sales generated) between 1987 and 1993.

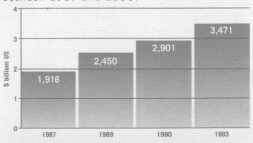

Fig 1.22 Travel and tourism output (Source: WTTC)
Source: Youell, R. (1995) Leisure & Tourism, Longman GNVQ

The growth in total world tourist arrivals 1970–93 is illustrated in Table 1.5.

Table 1.5 World international tourist arrivals 1970–93
Source: Youell, R. (1995) Leisure & Tourism, Longman GNVQ

Year	Arrivals (million)	Rate of growth (%)
1970	165.8	15.5
1971	178.8	7.9
1972	189.1	5.7
1973	199.9	5.1
1974	205.6	3.4
1975	222.3	8.1
1976	228.8	3.0
1977	249.2	8.9
1978	267.1	7.1
1979	283.1	6.0
1980	287.8	1.7
1981	290.1	0.8
1982	289.5	-0.2
1983	292.7	1.1
1984	320.2	9.4
1985	329.6	2.9
1986	340.6	3.3
1987	366.7	7.7
1988	420.0	9.6
1989	431.2	7.3
1990	458.4	6.3
1991	456.7	-0.4
1992	481.6	5.4
1993	500.1	3.9

Apart from the early 1980s and 1990s, when the world was experiencing recession, Table 1.5 indicates a steady growth pattern over two decades, culminating in more than 500 million tourist arrivals worldwide in 1993.

The Trend in Overseas Visitors to Britain

Figure 1.23 shows that, despite the world recession of the early 1980s and the downturn in the economy in the late 1980s, together with the lingering effects of the Gulf War (1991), the numbers of overseas visitors to Britain showed healthy growth between 1981 and 1993 (the latest year for which figures are currently available).

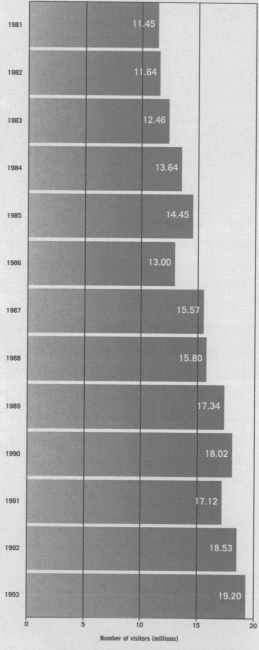

Figure 1.23 Overseas visits to Britain 1981–93 (BTS figures)
Source: Youell, R. (1995) Leisure & Tourism, Longman GNVQ

Task 2: The language used for incorporating data

Look back at the text on pages 67–68. Find and highlight the language used in the text to refer to the figures and tables, e.g. 'See Figure 1.21' (page 67).

Task 3: Figures and tables

Look at the examples of data on pages 70–71 (Data i–iv). They include two tables, a graph and a bar chart.

3.1 Identify whether each piece of data is a figure or table and label it appropriately, e.g. Figure 1 or Table 1.

3.2 The two captions below match two of the pieces of data i–iv. Identify which they are:

a) Radio listening: by age and gender, 1998

b) Subscription to satellite and cable television: by social class of head of family 1998–99

3.3 Copy the captions, placing them in the correct position above or below the data (see pages 67–68).

3.4 Now think of captions for the other two pieces of data and write them into the appropriate place.

3.5 Read the text below, and make reference to each sample of data at a suitable place in the text. One example has been added for you (see highlighted text below).

LIFESTYLES AND SOCIAL PARTICIPATION

According to the Family Expenditure Survey, by 1998–99, 13 per cent of households in the United Kingdom were subscribers to satellite television, and 9 per cent subscribed to cable television. Subscription to satellite is more common than cable among the majority of social groups, especially for households headed by skilled manual people, followed by households headed by managerial, technical and professional people. Despite the increasing number of television channels in recent years, the proportion of people listening to radio has remained fairly stable, with about nine in ten people in Great Britain reporting listening in the four weeks prior to interview in the General Household Survey in 1996–97. **According to the broadcasting industry survey,** overall people spent an average of 16 hours per week listening to radio in the United Kingdom in 1998. Listening to music on home music systems is another popular leisure activity. The dramatic rise in the sales of CDs in recent years has been accompanied by falls in the sales of cassettes and LPs. Many people also enjoy reading as a leisure activity. More daily newspapers, national and regional, are sold per person in the United Kingdom than in most other developed countries, although the proportion of people reading a national daily newspaper in Great Britain has fallen since the early 1980s.

Adapted from: Matheson, J & Summerfield, C (eds) (2000), Social Trends 30 2000 edition: The Stationery Office

---

(i)

	Males (%)				Females (%)			
	1971	1981	1991	1998–9	1971	1981	1991	1998-9
The Sun	26	31	25	24	15	23	19	17
The Mirror	38	27	20	15	29	22	15	12
Daily Mail	13	13	10	12	10	11	9	12
Daily Express	28	16	8	6	20	13	8	5
The Daily Telegraph	10	9	6	6	7	7	5	5
Daily Star	N/a	13	8	5	N/a	8	4	2
The Times	3	3	3	3	5	2	2	
The Guardian	3	3	4	3	3	2	2	2
The Independent	N/a	N/a	3	2	N/a	N/a	2	1
Financial Times	3	3	2	2	2	1	1	1
Any national daily newspaper	N/a	76	66	60	60	68	57	51

Source: National Readership Surveys Ltd

(ii)

United Kingdom	Hours and minutes per week		
	Males	Females	All
4–14	5:13	6:42	5.57
15–34	18:11	15:14	16:45
35–64	19:56	16:39	18:15
65 and over	16:54	17:34	17:18
All aged 4 and over	16:42	14:59	15:50

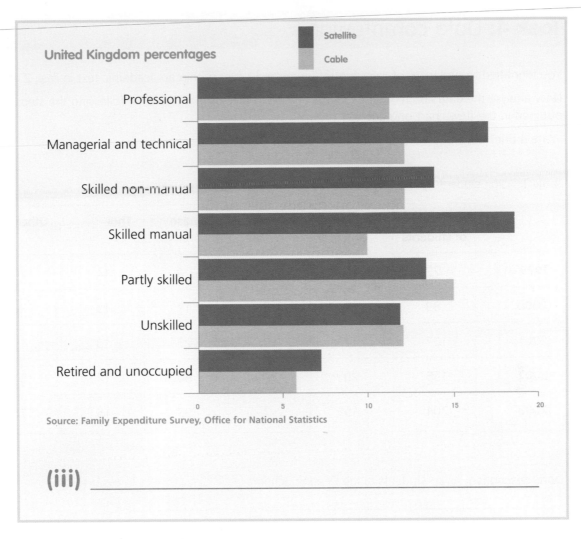

Source: Family Expenditure Survey, Office for National Statistics

(iii) _____

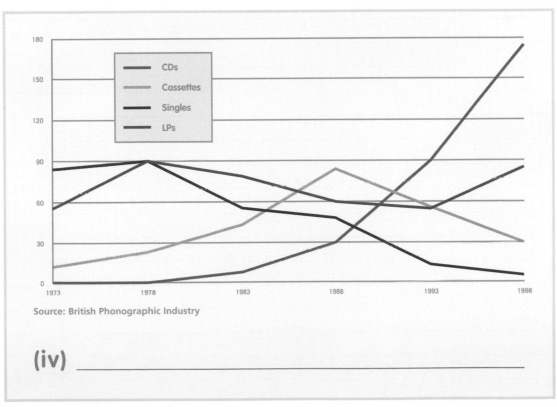

Source: British Phonographic Industry

(iv) _____

Task 4: Data commentary

You identified several ways of referring to figures and tables within an academic text in Task 2 above.

Now analyse the data about Asian students at the Oceanic School (Table 1), following the steps outlined in the flow chart on page 73.

Write a brief description of the data in the space provided below.

Table 1: Asian students at the Oceanic School

	Total number of students	Taiwanese	Japanese	Chinese	Thai	Other
1999	73	15	15	9	14	20
2000	89	12	15	17	15	30
2001	107	17	9	23	13	45
2002	155	20	7	60	17	51
2003	204	19	7	93	15	70

Data description: Asian students at the Oceanic School

Data commentary flow chart

Follow these steps when carrying out data commentary:

STEP ONE

Comment on the *subject* of the data.

↓

STEP TWO

Make a general comment on the *main trend*.

↓

STEP THREE

Comment on some of the *significant features*.

↓

STEP FOUR

If appropriate, *compare/contrast* various aspects of the data.

↓

STEP FIVE

Discuss the data. You might look at the implications or the reasons for some of the trends suggested by the data. This should be based on evidence.

Task 5: The language of data commentary

There are some key words that constantly appear in descriptions of data. These include a core pool of words that can be used as either verbs or nouns. The vocabulary is most often used in relation to data that is presented visually, e.g. bar charts or trend graphs. You need to be careful about the language structure in each case – it depends on whether you use the word as a verb or noun.

5.1 Look at the table below, and complete Columns A and B as far as possible by identifying the word forms.

Column A: Nouns	Column B: Verb forms	Column C: Accompanying adjective/adverb
rise		• • rose steadily
	increase/increased/ has increased	• dramatic increase • increased rapidly
fall		• • fell dramatically
drop		• •
decrease		• •
	stabilise	• remained stable •
fluctuation		• •

There is also a core pool of words used to make descriptions more precise. These are adverbs and adjectives and can be used, to say whether a change was, for example, sudden or predictable.

For example:

Between 1999 and 2002, there was a **dramatic** rise in the number of Chinese students studying in the UK.

5.2 Choose the most appropriate adjectives from the box below to complete Column C of the table. Some examples have been done for you. What changes should be made to each adjective to make an adverb, e.g. steady > steadily?

steady	dramatic	rapid	slow	dramatic
significant	expected	unexpected		noticeable

5.3 List other adjectives you could use to collocate with the nouns and verbs in Columns A and B of the table.

Collocations

_____

_____

_____

_____

_____

_____

_____

_____

_____

Task 6: Practice data commentary

Now write a data commentary on the information below comparing employment trends in the service and manufacturing industries. Use the five steps suggested on page 73, as well as some of the language from Task 5.

Figure 1: Employee jobs: by industry and sex (June each year)

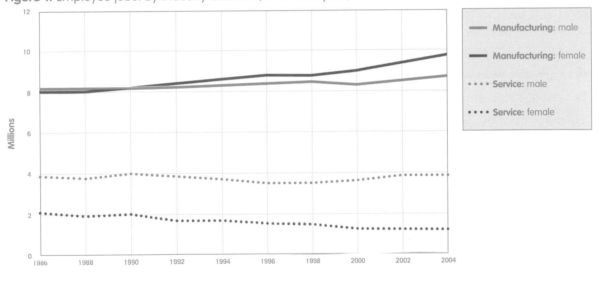

Source: National Statistics Online 2004 (adapted)

_____

_____

_____

_____

_____

_____

_____

8 Preparing for presentations and editing your work

In this unit you will:
- analyse and evaluate abstracts;
- write an abstract for (a) your project and (b) a conference presentation;
- prepare for an oral presentation using note cards and OHTs or PowerPoint®;
- learn how to prepare a poster presentation;
- edit the final draft of your project.

Writing abstracts

You may find it useful to look back at Unit 4 (pages 45–48) to remind yourself of the purpose of writing an abstract and the typical features of abstracts.

An abstract is a short summary of a whole project. It differs from an introduction, which may outline the structure of a project, but does not include findings or conclusions.

Abstracts may appear at the beginning of pieces of academic writing, for example, at the front of an academic journal. They also appear in conference programmes. The purpose in both cases is to give either the reader or the conference delegate a brief overview of the contents of the article or presentation. The reader or delegate can then make an informed decision about whether that text or presentation is going to be of interest to them. Usually there is a word limit for the abstract of a conference programme, which you should check carefully.

Written project abstract

You are now going to write an abstract for the beginning of your own written project. It can be most effectively written when you have completed the first draft of your project. The length of an abstract can vary; for a 3,000-word essay an abstract of 100–150 words would be appropriate. Remember to include some of the features below.

a) a general statement

b) essential background information

c) the aims of the project

d) an investigation into a particular topic or subject area

e) the implementation of the investigation in a real-world situation

f) how the text is organised

g) details of the research carried out by the writer

h) what the results of the research suggest

i) a thesis statement

j) a definition

Task 1: Features of abstracts

Look at the two sample abstracts from a written project, below, and identify any features from the list on page 76. Tick (✓) the table below.

ABSTRACT A

The evolution of foreign management consultancy firms in Italy and China: an evaluation of their localisation processes

Management consultancy has been developing for more than one hundred years. It originated in the United States, before spreading to other countries. Localisation plays an important role in the expansion of management consultancies. This, according to Crucini (1999), is the process of "adapting and translating management tools and ideas to work in a foreign market with a different economic or social background". The history of the spread of management consultancies is first described, followed by an outline of the localisation processes of foreign management consultancy firms in Italy and China. Some common problems encountered in the processes are then identified. Finally, advice is given on how to achieve successful localisation. (110 words)

ABSTRACT B

The manufacturing industry in the Mexican economy: a competitiveness model

In Mexico, the meaning and use of the term 'competitiveness' has evolved significantly in recent times. The lack of agreement among Mexican economic agencies about the meaning of the term partially explains the economic situation in recent decades, and has been a core problem in industrial policy. This paper proposes a model to assess competitiveness, and explain its complex meaning. First, it reviews some important economic concepts from the literature. Then, the relevance of the industrial sector in the Mexican economy is explained. Next, the model is applied to a specific situation in the manufacturing industry. The main conclusion is that this simple concept could be the beginning of a more sophisticated tool for implementing industrial policy in Mexico. (119 words)

Feature	Abstract A	Abstract B
a		
b		
c		
d		
e		

Feature	Abstract A	Abstract B
f		
g		
h		
i		
j		

Task 2: Practice abstract

2.1 Write an abstract for your written project in the box below. Write inside the box only. Try writing your abstract from memory – without looking at your project.

2.2 Exchange your abstract with a partner – which features can you identify in their work?

Abstract for written project

_____
_____
_____
_____
_____
_____
_____
_____
_____

Task 3: Conference abstracts

If you are participating in a conference, you will need to write a short abstract, for example 60 words, to appear in the programme. It will summarise the contents of your presentation.

Before you write a conference abstract, you need to decide which aspect of your project you will focus on. The time you have to give a presentation is limited, so you will not be able to include everything. The next three tasks look at some examples of conference abstracts, and factors to consider when preparing for your presentation.

Look at abstracts A–F. Match the abstracts to the following titles:

- Banking systems and management: challenges facing Taiwanese banks.
- Foreign investment in China
- Communication management in Transmission Control Protocol (TCP)
- Interpretation and analysis of financial statements for non-accountants
- Mixed-use developments in the Kingdom of Saudi Arabia
- Situation analysis in marketing

ABSTRACT A _____

Analysing the marketing situation is the first step that companies have to take when they make a marketing plan. This paper will describe the three frameworks of situation analysis and outline how Japanese frameworks compare with Western company frameworks. (39 words)

ABSTRACT B

Financial statements can be used as a tool for decision-making, planning and control by various user groups. The objective of this presentation is to describe how to globally transmit annual reports to non-specialist groups in accounting. Currently, some countries, including Thailand, are facing economic crises. This is owing to businessmen and women not properly understanding the meaning of financial statements, and making poorly informed decisions for their corporations. (68 words)

ABSTRACT C

This presentation explains the basics of computer networks and Transmission Control Protocol (TCP). It discusses the behaviour of TCPs in abnormal events as connections are being opened. Following this, normal closing processes and abnormal situations are explained. Finally, a Finite-State-Machine-Model is used to illustrate the status of the TCP unit during opening or closing of connections. (56 words)

ABSTRACT D

In the history of urban development, the use of the land in one relatively discrete area for a variety of purposes, for example, for residences, trade, employment and entertainment, has often been practised. The evolution of mixed-use developments was based on the idea of compact land use developments in areas with overgrown populations. This practice of mixed-use developments will be discussed with reference to the Kingdom of Saudi Arabia. (68 words)

ABSTRACT E

Since 1997, China has made a great improvement in its economy, and has become the economic centre of Asia. Foreign investment is the most obvious contributor to this performance, and has encouraged China's economic development. The purpose of this project is to analyse the investment environment in China, particularly the development and impact of foreign investment. (56 words)

ABSTRACT F

In an economic system, banks not only facilitate the matching of funds between savers and investors, but are also the main institutions for executing monetary policies. These policies need to be evaluated, and the 'CAMEL' model is one of the most effective ways to assess banking performance. This presentation attempts to evaluate the five criteria on which the 'CAMEL' model is based, and then applies them to the Taiwanese system of banking. (72 words)

Task 4: Practice conference abstract

4.1 Practise writing a conference abstract based on your project in the box below. Keep your abstract as brief as possible (maximum 60 words).

Abstract for conference presentation

_____

_____

_____

_____

_____

_____

_____

_____

4.2 In small groups and/or with your teacher, edit and discuss each other's abstracts. Pay attention to the typical features of abstracts and discuss content and language.

Task 5: Preparing an oral presentation

There are various ways of remembering what you want to say, and the order you want to say it, when giving a presentation. For example, some presenters prepare note cards on which they write down the main points of their presentation in the order they are going to discuss them. They write the notes clearly with lots of space between each point and arrange the note cards in numerical order. Good presenters do not read their notes aloud – they just use them as a way of reminding themselves of what to say.

Look at the following example of a note card prepared by a student who is going to give a presentation on International Relations.

CAUSES OF THE COLD WAR

a) Decline in relations – United States/Soviet Union

b) Nuclear arms race

c) Results of World War II

5.1   Discuss the note card on page 80 with a partner. In what ways is it useful for the presenter?

5.2   Look at the following presentation titles, which were chosen by students on a pre-sessional course:

- The retail trade in China: why native enterprises often fail
- Modern migration and its economic impact
- The causes and effects of climate change in recent years

Prepare a set of note cards on one of these topics that will give you enough information to speak for two minutes.

A PowerPoint® slide or overhead transparency (OHT) can be used as a stimulus for memory in the same way as a note card. However, such visual aids are mainly used as a way of clearly illustrating the key points of the presentation to the listening audience.

PowerPoint® should be used to present your ideas when possible. For practice in designing effective PowerPoint® presentations, go to **http://www.englishforacademicstudy.com**.

5.3   Below is an example of an OHT that might be used by the student who wrote the extended essay 'Remembering and forgetting: to what extent can we improve memory?' (Appendix 1).

Discuss the OHT with a partner.

a)   In what ways is it similar to a note card?

b)   How is it different?

Remembering and Forgetting

A. Definition
'Memory is one of the higher brain functions, and is crucial to normal functioning of the mind and to the phenomenon of consciousness.'
(Cohen, D. 1996, p.89)

B. Relationship between remembering & forgetting
- Importance of memory
- Reasons for memory loss

C. Improving the memory

Preparing a poster presentation

The purpose of a poster is to present ideas clearly and concisely. The main point of a poster should be immediately clear to the audience when they first see it, so you need to think carefully about the impact. Make sure you are selective – if you try to communicate too many ideas on a poster, your main idea will be lost.

Sketch it out!

● Make a sketch of the poster, using an A4 sheet of paper.

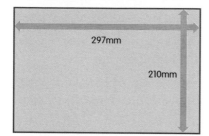

● Arrange the contents in a series of 3, 4 or 5 columns.
This will facilitate the flow of people past the poster.

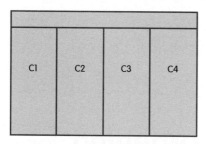

● Put the elements of the poster in position.

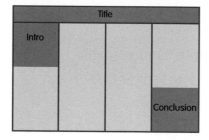

The title will appear across the top.
A brief introduction (3–5 sentences) will appear at the upper left.
The conclusions will appear at the lower right.
Method and results will fill the remaining space.

Guidelines for designing a poster

> ● It should have a strong visual impact.
>
> ● Ideas should be clear and comprehensive.
>
> ● It should be easy for the audience to follow.

Editing your written work

Very often, students work to deadlines and they hand in tasks at the last moment. Two hours spent on editing your work can make all the difference between creating the impression of a sloppy, careless piece of work, and one that is thoughtful and well-executed. Below are some guidelines to use as a checklist.

Title page	See example below*
Headings	Headings are a way of guiding the reader through your text. Make sure you have used enough of them. Make sure they are appropriate and numbered correctly (if you are using numbers).
References	Make sure you have acknowledged any ideas you have used from sources. Check each reference thoroughly, to ensure you have worded it in the correct way (author's surname, date).
Bibliography	Check that your bibliography is arranged according to academic convention. Make sure it is in alphabetical order.
Language	If possible, exchange your project with a classmate and proofread for each other, to make sure each section can be clearly understood. It is often easier to identify another person's language errors than it is your own.
Linking of ideas	Check that each section is related to the previous one and the next one.
Introduction and conclusion	Check your introduction and conclusion. Is each one linked to your title?
Feedback	Check the feedback from your tutor on previous drafts of your project. Have you reacted to this feedback appropriately?

● An example title page

UNIVERSITY OF READING

CENTRE FOR APPLIED LANGUAGE STUDIES
PRE-SESSIONAL COURSE BLOCK X 2003

Learner Independence and Self-Evaluation

Li Wang

Tutor: Peter Granger
September 2003

APPENDIX 1: Sample project

Remembering & forgetting:

to what extent can we improve memory?

Elton Mwila

PRE-SESSIONAL COURSE

Centre for Applied Language Studies

The University of Reading

University of Reading

Table of Contents

Abstract 1

Introduction 2

Remembering 3

Forgetting 5

How to improve memory 6

The relationship between remembering and forgetting 7

Conclusion 9

Bibliography 10

Abstract

Human memory is similar to computer memory; however, there is one vital difference – humans are unable to automatically retrieve every memory at the press of a key or the click of a mouse. Much effort is being made to improve human memory. This project sets

5 out to examine the reasons for memory loss and how it can be remedied. The conclusion will suggest that methods exist for improving human memory.

1

Introduction

"Memory is one of the higher brain functions, and is crucial to normal functioning of the mind and to the phenomenon of
10 *consciousness … it glues together fragments of consciousness, allowing people to construct narratives of their lives",*
(Cohen, 1996, p. 84).

In everyday life, people obtain a lot of information, and then they remember it and use it to settle problems. This is using memory. Memory is a faculty that helps people to
15 remember information. People cannot do anything without memory because it is one of the most important parts of life. Memory is like a computer; it can get information, store it, and when people want to use it, memory can retrieve it, so it is used to remember old and new information. However, nobody can recall everything; every second, people forget information, so a lot of people want to develop their memory.
20 People are increasingly looking for more effective ways to improve their memory skills, because they can use memory to study and live. Nowadays, psychologists and neurologists pay more attention to memory as they try to find the characteristics of memory and the biological factors involved.

This essay will describe what remembering and forgetting are, the relationship between
25 remembering and forgetting and how to improve the faculty of memory.

2

Remembering

Remembering is one of the most important parts of people's lives because the brain is constantly making use of both new and old information. Without memory people cannot study, work or do other things, so remembering is a basic human activity.

At first, if people want to remember a piece of information, they should obtain the
30 information, and when this information goes into their brains, it is registered by the senses – this is known as 'recognition'. After the brain has identified the features of the object and analysed them, it attempts to create a perceptual model. In addition, when the perceptual model is complete, the brain will search for other features, so this process keeps on recurring. Recognition is an elementary stage, and the perceptual model is an advanced stage memory.
35 This means recognition needs to be upgraded to the perceptual stage (Cohen, 1990).

Therefore, every day a lot of information comes to people's brains, and after a short time they cannot remember all the information. People have the skill of being able to remember some data for 1 to 4 seconds, but after that time, they may forget the data, so it has to be repeated. For example, people can remember a simple telephone number and then dial it,
40 but after the phone call, they forget the number – this is called 'short-term' memory (STM). Much of the information in STM is received acoustically, and STM keeps the information temporarily. After people use the data, it will disappear from their consciousness. STM can hold between five to nine items of information (usually it is seven items), which means people can repeat seven or eight items correctly immediately, but the capacity of STM is not
45 very large, and it is easy to forget. If people want to remember it well, they should repeat the information over and over. In addition, psychologist Alan Baddeley found that there are three ingredients in STM: one is articulatory loop in which sounds are remembered in two seconds; another is visual information, which is stored for five seconds; the third one is a central manager "that coordinates the total activity of the STM" (Cohen, 1996, p. 86).

50 STM can store information for a short time, but it is not enough for people to remember. Thus, there is another kind of memory called 'long-term' memory (LTM). LTM can store a piece of information for a long time – for hours, or even years. The difference between

3

long-term memory and short-term memory is: for short-term memory people obtain the information from the sound, but they do not understand, they just repeat the information;
55 long-term memory works by the meaning of the data, rather than by the sounds. For example, people can read a book to remember the meaning of the content, or they can listen to some information. Ultimately, they will find that it is easier to remember the meaning of information rather than the sound. In other words, if people want to keep the information in their brains for a long time, first they should understand it, and then remember it. The stages
60 of remembering can be summarized in Figure 1.

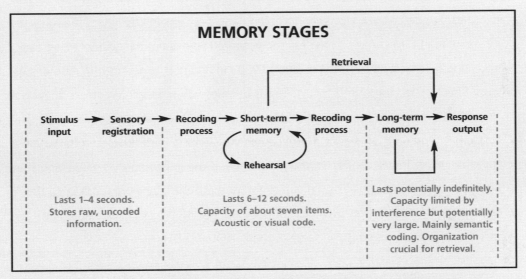

Figure 1: The modal model of memory (Source: Cohen, 1990)

This figure shows how information is obtained, stored and retrieved. Firstly, people see or hear information, which stimulates their brains, and then it goes to the sensorium, where the information is confirmed. The information is then stored in the brain. In addition, the information is unrefined at this time, which is why it can be stored in 1 to 4 seconds. Then
65 data enters the short-term store process. STM (as described above) contains information that at this stage is not necessarily understood; it is based on what people see or hear, so it lasts 6 to 12 seconds. If information wants to pass from short-term store into a long-term store, it needs to be rehearsed, which means to be repeated several times. Entering LTM, the stored time is indefinite, but after some time the information may be lost. Eventually, people can
70 use the information that is stored to answer or settle problems. However, real memory is much more complex than this model, because sometimes there are unexpected situations in daily life. Figure 1 just shows a simplified and fundamental procedure of memory.

4

Forgetting

When people remember information, maybe they can recall most of it, but forgetting is inevitable, so they can also lose information. The reason why people forget is because
75 they cannot use the whole of their brains. This happens in both STM and LTM.

There are two theories accounting for forgetting in STM: the 'trace decay' theory and the 'interference' theory. However, forgetting also happens in LTM, even though information in LTM can be stored for a long time. There is no real evidence that can explain why forgetting happens (Cohen, 1990). In addition, when information passes
80 from STM to LTM, forgetting occurs. This is because when people want information to stay in their memories for a long time, they practise or 'rehearse' it (see Figure 1) several times, but sometimes it is difficult to keep practising for a long time, so information is forgotten every few seconds. On the other hand, if the information is something that people habitually use, it is less difficult to forget, because they always use it, so the
85 speed of forgetting slows down, so from 24 hours to 48 hours the percentage of re-learning trials required is the same (Cohen, 1990, p.581).

5

How to improve memory

In life, remembering is very important, but forgetting also happens. Remembering and forgetting are virtually identical. Some people think remembering is a little difficult, but this depends on the individual. However, people can still find some successful ways to
90 improve their memories. Memory is selective. People can easily remember information that they use or need on a regular basis. However, in real life, people are often required to remember information that is important but may not be used by them frequently. This kind of data brings more difficulty, and people need to find a suitable way to retrieve the information. For instance, below is a list of words:

cabbage	parrot	red	spinach	carrot	read

95 These words may be quite difficult to remember in the very short term. But if people pay more attention to this list, they will find that cabbage and spinach have a common meaning, (i.e., vegetable) and that, although the first letter of the words carrot and parrot are different, the other letters are the same. Through carrot they will remember the colour red; and if they say the words aloud, they will also find red is pronounced in
100 a similar way to read. Through this association of ideas it will become easier to remember the group of words. During this process, people use 'vision' – the information that they see; 'hearing' – what they hear; 'comprehension' – meaning; and all of these belong to 'memory representation'. In addition, between the 17th and 18th centuries, the British philosophers Locke, Berkeley and Hume found that if objects or
105 concepts appear or occur concurrently, people can connect and remember them together, and so associating information will help them to obtain and memorize more data (Cohen, 1990). Therefore, when people want to remember more information, they can make use of all the memory.

6

The relationship between remembering and forgetting

After people obtain information, the most important thing is to remember it, but
110 nobody can recall everything. Every day there is a lot of old or new knowledge entering
people's memories, but as memory is selective, people forget information at the same
time, so some people think all forgetting is failing to remember. In addition, research
shows that the "… brain contains a permanent record of all experiences (the stream of
consciousness) and any forgetting is simply due to retrieval failure" (Parkin, 1993, p.67).

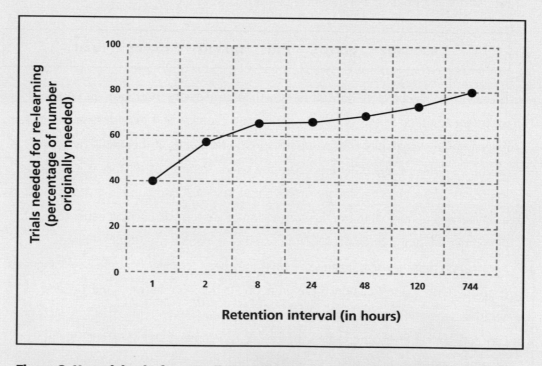

Figure 2: How delay before recall can influence forgetting (Source: Cohen, 1990)

115 Figure 2 shows in percentages the number of times facts need to be re-learned; for
example, if someone makes ten attempts to remember a piece of information and five
attempts to re-learn it, it means the amount of re-learning required is 50 per cent. A
number of re-learning attempts are required after 120 hours. Notice that at first, the
speed of forgetting is very quick, in fact, most forgetting happens in the first hour.

7

120 Moreover, 'practice' is also significant, because it helps people to adapt knowledge for themselves, in order to remember information consistently. Therefore, after some time, people should go through information again. During that time, they should not just repeat the information, but relate it to information that they already know well. People should also link abstract knowledge and concrete information together (Greenfield,
125 1999, p.167). For example, if a person wants to buy some things for his kitchen, he can recall these things one by one and go to the shops to find them, but there is a lot of information in his mind, so it would be easy to forget. He could just remember the shape of the kitchen in his brain, and when he goes to the shops, he imagines a picture of the kitchen: the knife is on the chopping board, the seasonings are in the cabinet,
130 etc. Therefore, it is much easier for him to remember things, because he changes the abstract information to concrete information, and he just needs to remember one object. In this way, it is possible to recall information more easily.

Memory representations have been mentioned before (in the context of using them to memorize information), but there is another way to practise, which is by using
135 'mnemonic devices'. Mnemonic techniques "weave together disparate bits of information into a meaningful sentence or into a story" (Cohen, 1996, p.86). People use mnemonic devices to remember pieces of information that are unconnected; for instance, in geography class, students are asked to remember the names of the North America Great Lakes (Huron, Ontario, Michigan, Erie, Superior), so they use the
140 acronym HOMES to help remember them (Cohen, 1996, p.86). Therefore, a mnemonic device is a particular method to remember information; before memorizing, people should understand the meaning of the information, and then find the relationship between each piece of information. After that they can create an effective mnemonic device and use that method to help them remember.

8

Conclusion

145 In conclusion, every day a lot of information goes into people's brains, so they have to remember a great deal of information. There are two kinds of memory: STM and LTM, and people can use these categories of memory to store different knowledge. If people do not need the data in their future study or life, they can keep the information in STM, which means they do not need to repeat it over and over. If they think the

150 information is very useful, and they want to keep it for a long time, they can choose LTM, but in this case, people should rehearse or practice. However, forgetting also happens in both STM and LTM. Regardless of what measures they take, people still lose information every few seconds.

Some people think that failing to remember cannot be remedied, but this is not true.

155 People can still find some suitable ways to improve their memories, such as repeating information several times or using mnemonic devices. If people work hard and they also have a good method, they will find remembering becomes much easier.

Bibliography

- **Cohen, D.** (1996) *The secret language of the mind*. San Francisco: Chronicle Books

160 - **Roth, I.** (ed.) (1990) *Introduction to Psychology*. Milton Keynes: Open University Press

- **Greenfield, S.** (ed.) (1999) *Brainpower: Working out the Human Mind*. Shaftesbury, Dorset: Element Books Limited

- **Norman, D. A.** (1982) *Learning and Memory*. San Francisco: W. H. Freeman
165 and Company

- **Parkin, A. J.** (1993) *Memory: Phenomena, Experiment, and Theory*. Oxford: Blackwell Publishers

- **Pollock, T.** (ND) *Ways to Improve your Memory* http://www.autofieldguide.com/columns viewed 11/06/03

10

APPENDIX 2: Self-evaluation checklist

Below is a list of the skills* you will need when working on extended pieces of writing during your university career. The work you do in this book, as well as on other aspects of your pre-sessional course, will help you develop these skills. Tick the appropriate box for each skill according to how well you feel you can do this. From time to time, look again at this checklist and decide whether you have made progress with any of these skills.

SKILLS	Do not know about this	Find this difficult/ cannot do this	Can partially do this	Can do this well
LOOKING FOR INFORMATION				
Identify which books/journals/ websites to use				
Select relevant parts of a text				
Evaluate sources				
USING SOURCES				
Acknowledge sources of information				
Synthesise information from more than one source				
Write a bibliography correctly				
PLANNING/WRITING				
Brainstorm ideas				
Plan written work				
Organise a text				
Link ideas effectively				
Summarise ideas				
Paraphrase ideas				
Write an introduction				
Write a conclusion				
Critically edit written work				
Avoid plagiarism				

SKILLS	Do not know about this	Find this difficult/ cannot do this	Can partially do this	Can do this well
PERSONAL STUDY SKILLS				
Work independently				
Manage time – meet deadlines				
ORAL EXPRESSION				
Give a presentation on my work				
Discuss ideas for project with other students				
Discuss written work in a tutorial				
IT SKILLS				
Access the Internet				
Use search engines				
Create Word® documents				
Use PowerPoint®				

* You may not require all the skills mentioned – there is some variation from department to department.

REMEMBER - A skill improves with practice!

APPENDIX 3: Taking notes

Why do you take notes?

- To record information.
- To help concentrate.
- To use as the basis of a summary.
- To use in essays.
- To help remember things.

Characteristics of good notes:

- They are accurate – the information record is correct.
- They are clear – you can read them weeks later.
- They are easy to understand – you know the connections you made.
- They are organised (e.g. highlighted or underlined) – you can identify the main points at a glance.
- They can be used for your specific purpose – you have enough detail for an essay, if that is what you need to write.

Task 1: Taking notes when listening or reading

What is the difference between taking notes when listening to a lecture or when reading an article? Fill in the table below with more differences.

Listening	Reading
You only hear it once, cannot rewind.	You can read it again and again.

Task 2: Discussion

What do you find most difficult about taking notes? Discuss with a partner and note your ideas in the table below.

When Listening	When Reading

Good strategies for taking notes

- Choose a note-taking style that suits you, e.g. mind mapping or linear.

- Think about your purpose before you write – why are you taking these notes?

- Use your own words as much as possible – this means you must understand what you read or listen to.

- Sometimes, it is more appropriate to annotate photocopied sheets or handouts or to use a highlighter pen or a pencil to underline key information. However, this makes it much more difficult to use your own words (or paraphrase the information) later.

- Be selective – only note down information that you think will be useful for your purpose, e.g. if you are looking for specific information to support a point in your project, you can ignore a lot of what is in the text.

- Give yourself plenty of space to write your notes, as you may want to add to them later.

- Use abbreviations (there are examples of these in Task 6, page 19). Make sure that you know what your abbreviations mean.

- When you have finished taking notes, look back and comment on what you have written. Write questions about the information/ideas, write down any connections or links with other notes you may have made. Be proactive when making notes as this will make them more meaningful.

Task 3: Note-taking strategies

Add any other note-taking strategies you know of below.

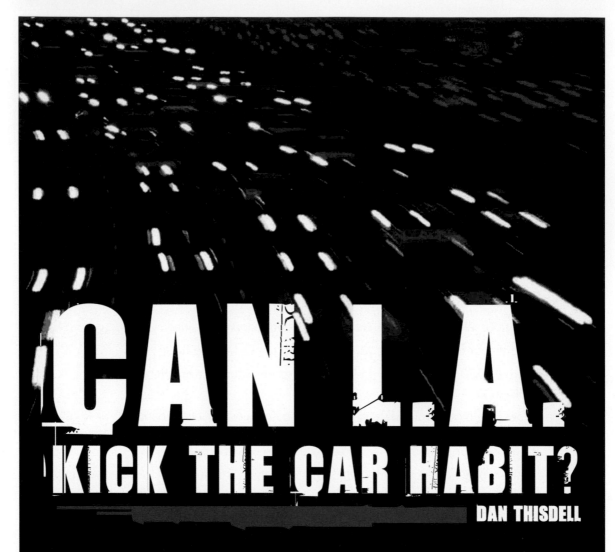

CAN L.A.
KICK THE CAR HABIT?

DAN THISDELL

For all its reputation as a trendsetter, Los Angeles stands out from other major cities such as New York, Tokyo, London, Paris and San Francisco through one glaring deficiency: it has never had an underground railway, and public transport of any kind has always been a rarity. But city planners believe it is the model for 21st-century American cities in the way it is becoming decentralised – and they are increasingly worried about how to curb people's reliance on their cars.

The first step was taken in 1993, when a 7-kilometre underground route with five stations opened from downtown Los Angeles to Hollywood. This Red Line was completed in 2000, and it is now 46 kilometres long, and is part of a 30-year effort to ease the region's chronic traffic congestion. The complete system, called Metro, will be an integrated network of underground and surface railways, shuttle buses and an improved freeway (motorway) system with new routes, high-technology aids to improve traffic flow, some toll roads, and "car pool" lanes reserved for vehicles carrying more than one person. Other elements of the Metro project include tow trucks patrolling freeways to clear crashed or broken-down vehicles, car parks at outlying rail stations, "dial-a-ride" services for the elderly and handicapped – and even expansion and improved maintenance of Los Angeles County's 800 kilometres of cycle ways.

The sea change of attitudes that Metro represents is hard to overstate. Los Angeles's physical appearance, size and society have been shaped during its rapid post-war growth by complete reliance on the private car. Railways have not figured in the transport equation until very recently. In 1990 the Blue Line, a 35-kilometre electrified rail service from Union Station to Long Beach, began running

Can L.A. Kick the Car Habit?

The sprawling Los Angeles city at dusk

45 along the route on which a similar service ran until 1961. By late 1992, three commuter lines started operating on existing freight tracks into the same terminal, where the underground begins. In the intervening three decades, the only public transport in Los Angeles County has been a bus network. It runs 25,000 buses and carries 1.3 million passengers daily, but much more is needed in a county that spreads over 11,340 square kilometres.

The Metro project is an attempt to reduce congestion and draw back some of the lost time and productivity, cut pollution and dependence on imported oil, and eventually improve the quality of life. But such dreams don't come cheap. The first short stretch of underground alone cost $1.45 billion, or about $200 million per kilometre. The alternative, though, is grim, for the scale of the problem facing the area is enormous. James Ortner, the air quality transportation administrator for the Los Angeles County transportation committee, says it is clear that road building alone can no longer meet the area's transport needs. An enormous public transport system, together with some expansion of the region's 960-kilometre freeway network, is now seen as the only way to stop traffic congestion getting even worse. With the population projected to grow as the region's inhabitants and their jobs become more scattered, traditional forms of public transport will be effective only in limited areas.

CAR CULTURE

The 8.8 million people living in the county of Los Angeles ten years ago owned six million motor vehicles. By 2010 the population is expected to exceed 10.2 million. But travel between counties in southern California is so significant that transport planning for Los Angeles County must also consider the surrounding counties such as Ventura and San Bernardino, an area of about 20,000 square kilometres. Its total population will probably climb to between 21 and 23 million by 2010 and the number of vehicle journeys each day will top 60 million – up from 45 million in 1990.

The population and physical area are combined with demographic trends and land-use patterns which make transport planning difficult. Unlike, say, London, which remains essentially a "mono-nuclear" region, with commuter travel patterns resembling a tidal flow to and from the centre each day, downtown Los Angeles is just the most significant of many centres in southern California. Despite being the focal point of Metro, the downtown area's dominance is expected to diminish in coming decades. Settlements around Los Angeles have always been widely dispersed; unlike European or American East Coast regions, they have never been tied to a dominant trading centre such as a port. Paradoxically, it was the railways which helped create this pattern. In the late 19th century railway companies were encouraged to open up the American west with offers of cheap government land. They built tracks and then sold on the surrounding land at a profit. This resulted in the early development of far-flung agricultural communities dispersed around Los Angeles (hence Orange County, where

Los Angeles freeway traffic

A cloud of smog covers the city

orange growers predominated) and meant that the inhabitants of Los Angeles were second only to Detroit – hub of the American motor industry 140 – in their haste to adopt the motor car early this century. The land-use patterns that make the private car so appealing to southern Californians have worked against 145 the establishment of a public transport system. The idea of an underground railway was proposed seriously in 1925, but the county's voters rejected the idea. As Ortner 150 points out, even then city dwellers in central Los Angeles who could have benefited from an underground were outnumbered by people from the rural communities, who 155 were already dependent on road transport.

Planners think that the population will grow fastest in suburban districts. The percentage of total employment 160 that is in downtown Los Angeles will fall, despite it being the one best served by public transport. There is a clear trend towards dispersal of both people and jobs to "edge cities" in 165 the county, meaning the continued creation of new centres of commuter travel. This problem is not unique to Los Angeles. Other American cities such as Chicago, New York, and 170 Houston are following a similar pattern. Ortner and his colleagues are therefore concerned to get the Metro programme working as effectively as

possible so that the lessons can be 175 applied more widely. However, the trend towards even greater dispersal can only make public transport more difficult to provide and less attractive to people with cars. Also, 180 reducing congestion on the freeways encourages car use, meaning that the proportion of journeys made on public transport falls. In the past decade in San Francisco, public 185 transport's share of the journeys made has fallen from 12 per cent to 8 per cent. The signs for Los Angeles are no more encouraging. "If we built every transit project on the books we 190 would still only have about 11 per cent of commuter trips on [public] transit in 2010," says Ortner. And he reckons that even if by then everyone was making the maximum use of 195 telecommuting – using telephone links to work from home – the figure would only grow to 13 per cent. Given the sums involved, the cost-benefit seems unsatisfactory. Ortner admits 200 that political considerations could ultimately remove the resources needed to achieve even that much.

The difficulty highlights two problems. One is that, in Ortner's words, 205 "the models which transportation planners have to work with are based on core-dominated urban regions of the 19th or early 20th century." But Los Angeles, and most 210 cities in the western US, are multi-nuclear areas, and the traditional

models do not work for them. "We're putting a round peg in a square hole," he says. There is an extra 215 twist which is probably not even unique to Los Angeles: it is that commuting is not the biggest problem. Nonwork trips – whether for leisure or as diversions from a 220 commuter journey (to drop children at school on the way to work, say, or to buy food on the way home) – at present account for a steady 80 per cent of all vehicle journeys. In 225 southern California, the worst day for air pollution is not during the working week, but on Saturday, when commuter traffic is negligible.

WRONG ROUTE

230 "For 30 years government money has been going on dealing with the commuter, and now we find that the nonwork trip is the biggest problem," says Ortner. "We don't know how to 235 handle it." In short, the well-cultivated freedom of movement that comes with cheap cars and low-priced petrol makes public transport an "inferior good". "I don't know how you fight 240 that," says Ortner. Los Angeles is thus a prisoner of its car-bound freeways; breaking free will entail changing life-styles. "The British should be forewarned," says Ortner. "If they want 245 to stop the [traffic] onslaught, now is the time to do it." Restrictions on the use of the road network might never be politically acceptable, but some steps will be taken. Ortner points to the 250 recent introduction of toll roads, a novelty in southern California, with "congestion pricing" which makes the roads more expensive at peak hours. More ambitious are plans to increase 255 the data capacity of the region's telephone system with fibre-optic cable to make it easier for people to telecommute. "Our goal is to redirect 20 per cent of future trips to home or 260 satellite work centres. It is too soon to tell whether or not that will work," says Ortner.

Can L.A. Kick the Car Habit?

Toll roads may be a way of reducing the congestion

The underground appears to have gone down well with the public. During its first week 21,000 people travelled on it each day – three times the projected number – helped by a one-week "introductory" flat fare of 25 cents. The figure fell in subsequent weeks, but the combination of existing and planned surface rail connections to Union Station and a network of local shuttle bus routes raises the hope of reasonably efficient commuting to downtown Los Angeles.

As a construction project, the underground is a large and challenging undertaking. One construction manager at a station that has yet to open describes it as the biggest civil engineering project now running in America; another calls it the eighth engineering wonder of the world. The hardest part about digging in any built-up city is to do it without causing major disruption on the surface. The tunnelling itself is relatively easy: just as with the Channel Tunnel or Thames Water's ring main around London, "mole" machines did the burrowing, producing tunnels 6–7 metres in diameter and 21 metres below the surface. Unlike the London Underground's labyrinthine networks of tunnels, the Los Angeles stations are simple concrete boxes. Designed with security in mind, they are equipped with video surveillance and patrolled by armed guards. There are no nooks, crannies or corners. A spokesperson for London Underground describes the system – like those in Washington and San Francisco – as being "built like tubes; since October eight motorists and and the stations are just bigger tubes." The designers were able to keep things simple because they were working from scratch on a system that only involves one line. Yet despite the emphasis on security, the platforms, entrances and exits are obvious targets for the criminal activity that is rife: 13 different gangs operate in a central section of the city, and defend their turf with guns.

Besides the human threats, there are two natural hazards: gas and earthquakes. Underground, the potential for methane explosions is a serious danger. The tunnels run through what Richard Seal, a senior construction inspector, describes as "very gassy" ground, where commercial oil drilling continued into the early 1900s. During construction, checks are made every four hours for gas, and the completed tunnels are lined with plastic 10 centimetres thick to keep the gas out. Because of the earthquake threat from the San Andreas Fault, they are also lined with concrete. The underground in San Francisco, which uses similar techniques, resumed service almost immediately after the October 1989 tremor, which measured 6.9 on the Richter scale and had its epicentre only 100 kilometres away.

One thing that cannot be built into a system is a "subway culture" of passenger etiquette and safety awareness. So far though, all seems orderly underground. On the surface, however, the level crossings for the Blue Line have caused some trouble: since October eight motorists and pedestrians have been killed after ignoring barriers. Several of the deaths are thought to have been suicides, but other victims may have been people not used to frequent passenger trains travelling at up to 100 kilometres per hour on lines until recently used only for freight.

Long-term funding for the underground is secure. In 1980 Los Angeles voters approved a half-cent sales tax on petrol, which raises about $400 million annually, of which 35 per cent goes to railway building. Another half-cent petrol tax approved in 1990 should raise another $400 million each year, specifically for the Metro project and highway improvements. What remains to be seen is whether the local culture can alter sufficiently to make public transport work. Legislation might help – for example repealing the local regulation which requires car parking to be made available as part of any development project – but the fear of crime may be the greatest obstacle. Economic uncertainty, the riots, especially in the early 1990s and the general scale of violent crime have left Los Angeles on edge. And though the underground hardly passes through the most crime-ridden part of the city, it does visit areas which many would rather avoid.

The search for a solution to Los Angeles's transport problems may turn out to be 'wishful' thinking. There may simply be no hope of changing the behaviour patterns of most long-distance car commuters. Ortner remains convinced that the effort is worthwhile, but admits that the decision made during the 1950s to rely on freeways and private cars has created a pattern of land use which will dominate Los Angeles for decades to come – possibly forever. "We will carry on through the fog and try to make life better for people," he says. "They may or may not want to use it. But: we can offer an alternative which will help … though it won't change land-use patterns all that much.

Source: Thisdell, D. (June 1993) *Can L.A. Kick the Car Habit? New Scientist*

SETTLEMENT CHANGES IN LEDCS

CASE STUDY URBANIZATION IN AFRICA

Towns and cities have existed in LEDCs for a long time. Since 1950, LEDC towns and cities have grown rapidly as people have moved from the countryside. Their pop-
5 ulations have also increased until recently, because of high birth rates.

Urbanization in LEDCs is different from that found in MEDCs in the speed and scale of change. The three main differences are that
10 population growth rates are higher, income levels are lower and the urban areas have weaker planning and administration to cope with the extra population.

The average percentage of the population
15 in urban areas is 37 per cent but it does vary. In Latin America the figure is 66 per cent, whereas in China and SE Asia it is only 25 per cent. In Africa the figure increased from 25 per cent to 33.4 per cent between 1990 and
20 1995. Africa has the most rapid rate of urban growth of population (C).

LEDC governments often encourage urban-ization, despite the problems caused, because, per person, they are three to four
25 times more productive than rural areas. However, dealing with the problems of urban areas often causes governments to neglect their rural people.

Experts think that the urban population of
30 Africa will have huge increases in the next few years. High fertility, fewer infant deaths and increasing life expectancy suggest the urban population could double by 2010. Cairo has already emerged as a mega-city with more than
35 12 million people in 1995, and Lagos is expected to soon.

Problems in large cities in Africa:

- High unemployment and large informal sector.
40 - Poverty.

- Poor quality and overcrowded housing.
- Failing transport, water supply and sewage systems, e.g. in Accra only 35 per cent of houses are connected to a sewage
45 system and only about 66 per cent of the solid waste produced by houses is collected. In Dar-es-Salaam 65 per cent is collected, in Kampala only 10 per cent.
- Water is often contaminated and there is
50 too little of it, e.g. in Accra only 35 per cent of houses have indoor piping of water, 24 per cent use a stand pipe and 28 per cent buy from water vending carts. The remaining houses collect rainwater
55 and use open waterways.
- Overcrowded education and health facilities.
- Rapid growth of a young population through migration from nearby smaller
60 towns and increasing life expectancy.
- Destruction of any free land in the urban area, especially along water courses, and the felling of trees for firewood.
- Inadequate enforcement of the law espe-
65 cially on the environment and health.

African cities with populations over 1 million

Geographical location	1970	1980	Examples
North Africa	4	8	Cairo (12m) largest in Africa. Algiers, Alexandria, Casablanca, Khartoum, Rabat, Tripoli, Tunis
West Africa	1	8	Ibadan, Jos, Kedina, Lagos, Abidjan, Accra, Conakry, Dakar
East Africa	0	6	Addis Ababa, Nairobi, Dar-es-Salaam, Harare, Lusaka, Kampala
Central Africa	1	6	Kinshasa, Kananga, Luanda, Maputo, Yaounde, Douala
Southern Africa	2	5	Johannesburg, Cape Town, Durban, Pretoria, Port Elizabeth

WHY HAS MEXICO CITY GROWN?

It is estimated that Mexico City (A) will have a population of nearly 20 million by the year 2000. Its population density is well over 10,000 people per sq km. Its population has been
5 growing rapidly because of the arrival of large numbers of migrants from the countryside, high birth rates and falling death rates. It is estimated that 40 per cent of its population live in 'informal settlements' or 'shanty towns'.

10   However, Mexico City is not all poor houses. The city has a long history with many magnificent buildings as well as broad highways flanked by multi-storey corporate headquarters. There is an extensive metro system within the built-up area,
15 an international airport and university.

One Internet site describes the city as 'crowded, polluted, and chaotic but also passionate, exotic and beautiful'.

1 Rural to urban migration

20 Factors that push people from the rural areas and factors that pull them to urban areas are listed in (D). About 1,000 new migrants arrive in Mexico City every day. Of course there are positive things about living in the countryside
25 and negative ones in the urban areas. The 'bright lights' of the urban areas make them more attractive than they really are.

Push factors	Pull Factors
Poverty	Richer people
Low pay	Better pay
Unemployment	More jobs
Few schools	Primary and secondary schools
Few doctors	Health care and hospitals
Poor roads	Cars
Poor electricity and water supply	Electricity and water
	Entertainment

In LEDCs migrants often move first to a local town and then to Mexico City. This is called 'step-wise'
30 migration. However, as birth rates remain high in rural areas and health care is improving, the population total in rural areas is not falling.

There are jobs in the cities – 65 per cent of Mexico's economic activity is in Mexico City. There
35 are oil, chemical and food processing industries. In addition cement, glass, paper, clothing, electronics, household appliances and cars are made in the city. Most of the main banks have their head offices here. The people of the city have very varied ways
40 of life. There are houses for the rich in elegant suburbs such as Pedregal (A) as well as crowded squatter settlements, such as Netzahualcoyotl, which is located on the dry bed of Lake Texcoco (A).

2 High birth rates

45 When the migrants arrive in Mexico City, they find life hard with little or no employment available. All the family
50 works to get money for food and to pay the rent for their tiny

room in a shanty town. Many children miss school, have a low level of education and many
55 girls are pregnant by their sixteenth birthday. Only 55 out of every 100 children attend primary school despite free education. Few know how to use contraception. Many of the people moving to the urban areas consist of younger age groups.
60 As a result birth rates are high (24 1998).

3 Death rates are falling

In the past, poor water supplies, little sanitation, rubbish and sewage in open drains meant that death rates were high, and buses have made
65 the air so polluted that to breathe is equivalent to smoking 25 cigarettes per day. The city planning authorities with the help of overseas aid, are improving health. They are investing in more doctors and hospitals; there are
70 restrictions on car use; they use lead-free petrol; a metro train has been introduced, and self-help housing schemes have been introduced. These actions improve the quality of life for people and the death rate caused by pollution has dropped
75 significantly (5 per 1000 in 1998).

There are signs that the growth rate of cities in LEDCs has improved mainly because, as women become more educated and they start to use contraceptive methods such as the birth pill, infant
80 mortality has decreased. In addition, in Mexico, other cities have started to grow rapidly.

PROBLEMS

Housing

In Mexico City, as in other LEDCs, housing is
85 seen as the highest priority. Unlike most cities in
MEDCs the houses of the poor are mostly found
on the edges of the city. These are often found in
unplanned, illegal settlements called 'shanty
towns'. Mexico City has become ringed by a
90 series of shanty towns – 'villages' – often built illegally but on public open space or even on
farmer's land. They are built from scrap materials
and are usually one-roomed shacks. They lack
the basic amenities of housing such as running
95 water and sanitation. Some houses have electricity by connecting illegally to the main supply,
which runs outside the town. No one knows how
many people live in the shanty towns.

Water, land and air pollution

100 Water pollution is a problem because rainwater is
not kept separate from industrial and domestic
users. This leads to the pollution of drainage channels. The high temperatures and heavy rainfall
make this worse. In some cities sewage is still
105 drained directly into rivers. Most shanty towns
have no sewerage system and use pits dug in
open spaces. On hillsides, such as those around
Rio de Janeiro, the sewage may seep down into
other people's drinking water supply. In Mexico
110 City only about 75 per cent of the rubbish is collected by the refuse collection service. In some
areas women collect human excrement to dump in
refuse pits nearby. Illegal dumping of industrial
waste and refuse from the 'informal sector' creates
115 land pollution. Because Mexico City is sited in a
basin surrounded by hills, the air pollution from
four million cars and industry is not blown away.
Car and bus fumes are a problem because of old
inefficient engines and low-quality petrol.

120 Subsidence

Parts of 'downtown' Mexico City are built on the
soft deposits of an old lake. Some areas have fallen
by 6m damaging buildings and breaking water
and sewerage pipes. New buildings have to be
125 erected using steel piles and concrete drums.
There have been suggestions that the conditions
in some areas of Britain are nearly as poor as those
found in LEDC cities. In areas such as South
Yorkshire the unemployment level is over 15 per
130 cent since the closure of steel works and coal
mines. Earnings are low and the amount of derelict
land is five times the national average. This is the
area where the film " The Full Monty" was made.

THE WAY FORWARD

135 Discourage rural to urban migration

The key thing to do is to improve conditions in
other areas so that people do not wish to migrate
for the apparent advantages of the city. This can
be done by providing employment in other areas
140 as well as by improving their educational and
social services. Better transport allows people to
live out of the city even if they commute in each
day. In Indonesia the authorities tried to ban
migration by issuing people with identity cards
145 and requiring permits to change residence.

Build satellite New Towns to disperse population

Hong Kong and Singapore have built high-density
housing to reduce their problems of housing
150 shortage. They could afford to build high-rise
blocks of flats in new settlements outside the city.
Kuala Lumpur used the same solution but built low-
rise four-storey blocks. In all three cases the new
residents were able to pay rents for their flats.

155 Increase employment

Tourism is a key area for the growth of jobs.
Tourists provide foreign currency that is vital to
countries' development. They demand many
services and this creates jobs. Many cities in
160 LEDCs have features that attract tourists. City
growth, increased traffic and neglect can threaten
these attractions, for example the historic colonial
core of Kuala Lumpur, the mangrove areas near
Santos in Brazil, the beaches of Rio de Janeiro
165 and the Taj Mahal in India. City authorities need
to publicize the importance of conserving these
important sites. A key feature of this strategy is to
involve local business people, schools and residents.
The 'informal sector' is being recognized as
170 one way to encourage employment. There are
two main types of informal employment:
- Services such as shoeshine boys, street
  vendors, repairers, newspaper sellers,
  unofficial guides and food and drink sellers.
175 • Small-scale manufacturers of pottery, crafts,
  soaps, traditional ornaments, etc.

The informal sector supplies everyday goods at cheap prices as well as meeting the needs of some tourists. The traders are usually operating
180 outside the law and without a license. In parts of India and Kenya the government has appreciated the role this group plays in growing trade and has given some protection to the people. The governments recognize that the informal sector
185 employs large numbers of people though conditions and wages may be poor. Unfortunately the informal sector has a reputation for employing children and illegal immigrants.

The sector is very adaptable and ready to try
190 to supply to most demands. Encouragement of this sector may lead to the growth of more stable industries and the money that changes hands fuels the economy of the city.

Provide self-help housing

195 These are schemes where the local authority provides a concrete base and water supply to a small plot of land. The owner, often helped by neighbours, builds a house for the family. A second floor may be added as the town gets
200 older. Gradually the self-built estates are upgraded as electricity is added.

Elect stable government

In many cities in LEDCs, bureaucracy, corruption and unrest, including terrorism, have not helped
205 to sustain the quality of life in the area. Foreign investors have to consider these problems when they consider where to locate their production plants. The low wages they would have to pay and the lack of trade union activity attract them
210 but they fear disruptions to production and the safety of key workers.

Improve transport

The government would like to encourage people to use public transport, but it has to have the
215 finance to fund new buses and rail routes. Some successes have been achieved in Hong Kong, Singapore and Malaysia where wealthier governments had the funding.

Obtain international aid to
220 ### repair infrastructure

Education, especially for women and children including the street children and homeless adults as well as the mentally ill, would reduce population growth and provide better skills to help with employment.

225 ### Introduce legal restrictions
and fines to reduce pollution

The Mexico City authorities have joined with the national government and PEMEX (the national petroleum manufacturer) to agree an eight-point
230 strategy costing 8 billion pounds. The eight points are as follows:
- checking car and bus exhaust fumes with restrictions on use until unleaded petrol used
- all new vehicles to be fitted with catalytic
235 converters
- fines for companies found disposing of waste by illegal means
- monitoring of human solid and liquid waste disposal especially on beaches and public
240 open spaces
- new cleaner technologies to be used in factories
- introduction of cleaner fuels
- education about environmental issues
- improved public transport.

245 ### Involve citizens

Local authorities have formed Citizens' Councils to involve local people. Similar movements exist in the UK as well. Local people are able to suggest the best ways forward to meet their needs.
250 Local authorities form Environmental Councils to:
- propose methods of preserving the local environment
- receive complaints about threats to open spaces and vegetation
255 - be a public voice influencing the City Council.

SETTLEMENT CHANGE IN EUROPE

In the EU there is a core of areas with high population density stretching, nearly continuously, from central and south-east England through to southern Italy. This contains most of the largest urban areas in Europe.

Europe was the birthplace of manufacturing industry. The manufacturing areas of Europe developed with the help of their own cheap coal. As late as 1962 only Italy and the Netherlands in Europe used more oil than coal. By 1972 oil had become the main energy source. Founded on the coal-producing areas of the UK, France, Belgium, Luxembourg and Western Germany, a broad zone of industry developed. London's population reached 1 million by 1810 and 2 million in 1850. Paris reached 1 million by 1850 and Berlin, Vienna and Moscow by 1900. By 1994 some 68 metropolitan areas had developed in Europe. The large urban areas of Europe are London, Paris, Randstad (Holland), Rhine-Ruhr and Moscow.

European urban problems

The successful growth of large urban areas also brings problems including:

- shortage of good quality housing, overcrowding and the creation of slums
- congested living in inner-city areas
- dangers of urban sprawl using up the countryside
- restless migrant populations
- long journey to work
- city transport system under strain
- widespread car ownership and traffic congestion
- need to renew central areas
- migration of people out of the tax area of the city they use.

Deurbanization

Since 1965, people have been leaving the urban areas of Europe to live in the semi-rural areas on the urban fringes. As a result the total populations of the large built-up areas have been falling. This has been made possible by improved transport which has made long-distance commuting, by better-paid people, a possibility.

There are many causes of deurbanization, including:

- increased life expectancy and longer retirements
- increased earned wealth of people retiring from urban employment
- decline of traditional heavy industry and textiles
- anti-urban feelings – viewed as crowded, congested, polluted, stressful as opposed to rural peace.

Reurbanization

In the 1990s a number of governments have become concerned about the decline of their urban areas and plan to make them more attractive.

Source: **Bilham-Boult, A. et. al. (1999)** *People, places & themes.* **Heinemann**

APPENDIX 4: Source 3

SOCIAL JUSTICE IN THE CITY

Inequality and conflict in the city lead to a
consideration of social justice in the urban
environment. Achieving a more equitable
distribution of accommodation and
5 services in the city is a desirable goal but
one that is difficult to achieve. Most city
authorities accept some responsibility
for the provision of public-sector housing,
although the degree to which they become
10 involved varies enormously from city to
city and from country to country. In their
different ways, urban planners in both
Hong Kong and the cities of the former
Soviet Union have seen social justice in
15 housing as one of their prime objectives.
The extent to which they have achieved
it will be studied in the two examples
that follow.

CASE STUDY:
Housing and the New Towns in Hong Kong

An extract from the Hong Kong Year Book, 1988, summarises the difficulties that exist in the provision of housing in the Colony and the New Territories.

'Despite the many modern buildings and other developments in Hong Kong, it cannot be denied that, as in any large city, there are run-down areas and other environmental black spots. This is not surprising, considering how rapidly Hong Kong's economy has grown. Some areas that were developed as recently as 30, or even 20 years ago were built to lower standards when the Territory was less affluent and have since deteriorated. In most of these run-down areas, there is severe overcrowding and a general lack of space for normal amenities.'

The population of Hong Kong was reduced to about 601,000 at the end of the Second World War in 1945, but by the end of 1947 an influx of people from mainland China had swollen the figure to 1.8 million. With the establishment of the Chinese People's Republic in 1949 further immigration from the north saw the population rising to some 2.2 million in 1950. This steady influx of refugees put intense pressure on housing. Squatter settlements began to appear around the edge of the urban area, on rooftops and in sheltered bays of the much indented coastline of the mainland and the island. The squatter communities still exist and are, to a large extent, tolerated by the government; special areas were created for some of the poorer families to build homes. Existing tenements saw a degree of subdivision which led to much overcrowding.

In 1953 a disastrous fire in a squatter settlement at Shek Kip Mei, Kowloon, left 53,000 people homeless and the government with no option but to house them. Shanties have remained, however and there is basically no systematic rehousing of squatters. They are only cleared when land is needed for redevelopment; land needed for future development is kept free of squatters and patrolled regularly. Squatters that are registered are rehoused; others are moved to temporary housing in which they can make their own improvements to what is essentially a bare shell.

Squatting has increased in junks and sampans in Hong Kong Harbour and in small creeks throughout the colony and the New Territories. The control of these boat squatters has proved to be a particularly difficult problem for the authorities. In recent years the arrival of refugees from Vietnam has exacerbated the problem. The long indented coastline of the colony and its islands makes total surveillance almost impossible. Squatters on boats regularly petition for public housing, but as soon as some areas are cleared, new arrivals appear and the problem returns.

The map (Figure 3.38) shows the principal squatter settlements that existed in 1955.

Figure 3.39 So Uk squatter village, Hong Kong

Public Housing in Hong Kong

There are essentially three phases in the development of public housing in Hong Kong.

85 ● **Phase 1** 1954–64. Initial rehousing of squatters from Shek Kip Mei (after the fire); acquisition of building land for redevelopment; big programme of high-rise public housing begins.

90 ● **Phase 2** 1964–73. Big expansion in public housing programmes; estates mainly developed on the periphery of the urban area. Planning for the new towns begins.

95 ● **Phase 3** 1974–present day. Reorganized housing authority has much wider powers; emphasis on the New Towns and the New Territories; first provision of government housing for middle-income families.

The move to the new towns

100 As the government housing plans gathered impetus, it became apparent that available space in the Kowloon Peninsula and the north shore of Hong Kong Island was rapidly becoming exhausted. If the population was to 105 be housed adequately, a radical solution had to be found. The only suitable land for future development was in the New Territories, beyond the central mountain barrier and around the eastern and western coasts. 110 Population nuclei already existed and it was to these small rural and coastal centres that the authorities looked to fulfill the next stage of their programme. However, if population growth was to be stimulated in the new 115 locations the problem of accessibility to the inner metropolitan areas would have to be solved. In the early stages of the development of the New Territories the majority of employment opportunities would still be on 120 the Kowloon Peninsula and Hong Kong Island. The success of the creation of the new towns in the northern and central New Territories would be tied to the development of a fast and efficient transport system cutting through 125 the central mountain complex. Such a service is provided by the fully electrified Kowloon-Canton Railway and the Mass Transit Railway (see Figure 4.47), which links Tsuen Wan into the metropolitan area and has three 130 lines, 36.6 km of track and 37 stations, with interchange facilities at five.

Table 3.16 – New Towns in the New Territories

New town	Present population	Target population	Transport link
Tsuen Wan	500,000	800,000	Mass Transit Railway
Sha Tin	300,000	750,000	Kowloon-Canton Railway
Tuen Mun	300,000	500,000	LRTS and Hovercraft
Yuen Long	110,000	180,000	LRTS and Hovercraft
TaiPo	150,000	290,000	Kowloon-Canton Railway
Fan Ling	110,000	220,000	Kowloon-Canton Railway

LRTS: Light Railway Transit System

SOCIAL JUSTICE IN THE CITY

Housing and the New Towns in Hong Kong

The present six New Towns are likely to be outpaced by the population growth in Hong Kong and the New Territories. The maximum
135 size of the largest (Tsuen Wan) is 800,000, and it is not thought desirable to exceed this figure. Three New Towns are required for second-generation population growth.

Table 3.17 – Five possible sites for New Town developments

Site	Physical geography	Existing settlements	Land use	Communications
Tin Shui Wai	Mudflats and low-lying surrounds: reclamation needed	Series of small villages involved in market gardening, fish culture and fish ponds	Mostly rice cultivation and market gardens. High environmental value of mudflats – wildlife much prized – nearby areas are protected	Nothing to prevent extension of Light Railway from Yuen Long and Tuen Mun. Rather isolated on north-west of New Territories
Ma On Shan	Low-lying floodable land on flanks of Tolo Harbour. Backed by high mountains rising to over 2,000 feet (702 m)	Small fishing settlements on Tolo Harbour	Mostly rice cultivation: some market gardens. Wildlife reserves; Ma On Shan Country Park	Main Kowloon-Canton railway on other side of Tolo Harbour. Possible link to Sha Tin New Town – road needs upgrading
Junk Bay	Deep inlet east of Kowloon. Flat land at north inland end: some reclamation possible	Two small fishing villages: Tseung Kwan O and Pennies Mill. Very close (2 km) to eastern suburbs of Kowloon	Mostly scrub-covered; some rice cultivation: wooded hills surrounding main inlet	Close to the suburban transport net of metropolitan Hong Kong. Possible extension of Mass Transit Railway
Nam Chung	Low-lying land around head. Starling Inlet – some reclamation will be needed. High wooded hills to north (Robin's Nest)	Small villages of Nam Chung, Wo Hang and Luk Keng	Mostly market gardening, fish ponds and duck ponds. Wooded hills surround	Good-quality road to Fan Ling on Kowloon-Canton Railway
Stanley Bay	Peninsula site: wooded hills to north, sloping down to Stanley Bay	Stanley Town – market centre and tourist attraction. Scattered settlements over hillsides: some shanty towns	Mostly wooded hills interspersed settlement, little cultivation	Tortuous route to north via Repulse Bay linked to main Aberdeen Road into Wan Chai and Causeway Bay

Source: Chaffey, J (1994) 'The Challenge of Urbanisation' in Naish and Warn (eds) Core Geography London: Longman pp. 138–146

SOCIAL JUSTICE IN THE CITY

Housing and the New Towns in Hong Kong

APPENDIX 4: Source 4

SUSTAINABILITY

W. M. Adams

I have long wanted to complain to Bill Gates that my word processor's spell-checker does not recognise the word 'sustainability'. At first this surprised me, for the word has become
5 indispensable in any discussion of human impacts on the environment. It is hardly one of those secret words only used by academics and other toilers in the depths of libraries, for it peppers the speeches of politicians, teachers,
10 business leaders and environmentalists and, of course, geographers.

But perhaps Microsoft's dictionary-compilers are not so behindhand, for in fact sustainability has only recently become so widely used. The ideas
15 for which it is so convenient (and, as we shall see, so slippery) a label have been around for many decades, but sustainability is very much a word of the 1990s. Specifically, it owes its global reach to the vast media roadshow surrounding
20 the United Nations Conferences on Environment and Development (UNCED, or the 'Earth Summit') at Rio de Janeiro in Brazil in June 1992.

That event brought together 128 Heads of State and 178 governments and their attendant
25 lobbyists, as well as a host of non-governmental organizations (Chatterjee and Finger, 1994). Sustainability was UNCED's 'Big Idea'. Thus launched upon the world, its meteoric rise to global buzzword began. But what does
30 sustainability mean? Why did it emerge at Rio? What use is it? These questions are rather harder to answer than they look.

WHAT IS SUSTAINABILITY?

What does sustainability mean? Irritatingly, we could answer, 'everything and nothing'. It is a word that promises much. A dictionary definition offers a range of meanings, each of which captures something of the meaning of sustainability. Longman's Dictionary of the English Language (1991) gives the following definitions of the verb 'to sustain':

45
- to give support or relief to;
- to supply with sustenance, nourish;
- to cause to continue, prolong;
- to support the weight of;
50
- to bear up under, to endure (to suffer, to undergo).

They are all to do with continuity ('prolonging', 'nourishing', 'supporting', 'enduring'). They are also all basically positive, all things that might be thought of as broadly desirable or admirable. In public debate about environment and development, use of the word sustainability suggests that change can be allowed to happen (or made to happen), that the best of what has been done before is maintained, whether that change is in an economy or society ('sustainable development') or in an ecosystem ('sustainable environmental management').

Internationally, the dominant definition of sustainable development has undoubtedly been that of the Brundtland Report, in *Our Common Future*: 'development that meets the needs of the present without compromising the ability of future generations to meet their own needs' (Brundtland, 1987: 43).

This definition is both rhetorical and vague (Lélé, 1991), but it proved compelling as a way of pulling together concerns about environmental degradation and present and future poverty (often spoken of as inter- and intra-generational equity).

The word sustainability first appeared in British legislation in 1991, in the Act establishing the conservation organization Scottish Natural Heritage (SNH). SNH was charged with achieving and promoting the conservation and enjoyment of landscapes and wildlife 'in a manner that is sustainable'. This apparent coup for environmental thinking caused some scratching of heads in the new agency, because while the word might have sounded wonderful in Parliament, its meaning was far from clear. Eventually, SNH suggested that sustainability should mean 'the ability of an activity or development to continue in the long term without undermining that part of the environment which sustains it' (SNH, 1993). While heart-warming (and arguably very wise) as a general principle, this is hardly a sharply focused definition. When other UK national conservation agencies set up in 1991 got in on the act, their own definitions were no more specific. Their definitions of sustainability and sustainable development were:

- The ability of an activity or development to continue in the long term without undermining that part of the environment which sustains it (Scottish Natural Heritage, 1993).

- Sustainable development seeks to improve the quality of human life without undermining the quality of our natural environment (English Nature, 1993).
- Sustainability implies that human use of or enjoyment of the world's natural and cultural resources should not, in overall terms, diminish or destroy them (Countryside Commission, 1993).

Summary

Sustainability is an emotive word, with complex meanings.

The concept of sustainability began to be used internationally in the 1980s (notably in the report of the Brundtland Commission in 1987), and first appeared in British law in 1993.

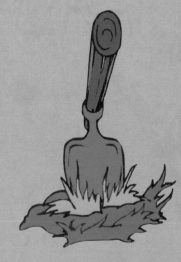

SUSTAINABILITY: MORE THAN A BUZZWORD?

The Council for the Protection of Rural England describe sustainable development as 'the latest buzz-phrase to hit the planning profession' (Jacobs, 1993: 8); indeed, it has become almost impossible to avoid using it. Geography has certainly not been free of its influence, as a glance round any mainstream publisher's catalogue, or a swift perusal of geography textbooks (including this one, of course!) would prove. Sustainability is therefore quite obviously important, if one measures something's importance by the number of people talking about it. What is less clear, however, is whether anything much lies behind the glittery promise of the word.

Superficially, the concept of sustainability seems very simple, yet it can have a wide range of meanings attached to it. Rio Tinto Zinc, or Shell, might speak of sustainability in the context of mineral extraction, but mean something very different to a Friends of the Earth campaigner or someone from Nigerian Ogoniland (see Fig 13.1); the Chancellor of the Exchequer might speak (indeed, has spoken) of 'sustainable' national economic management, and mean something very different to a proponent of a zero-growth economy (see Box).

Both environmentalists and conventional economic and political planners use the word sustainability to express their own vision of how economy and environment should be managed. The word does not end the debate about how society should exploit non-human nature, it simply re-labels it. Indeed, such is the power of sustainability to allow different ideas to be smuggled forward in its ample conceptual folds that it effectively delays debate and pushes it underground. Radical opponents of roads and other infrastructure have literally taken to the ground (or the trees) in opposition (see Figure 13.2). Their concerns have not been met by the growing debate about sustainability and transport in the UK. For a single

Figure 13.1 Ken Saro-Wiwa, Nigerian Ogoniland protester and playwright, killed by the Nigerian State in 1996 following protests about environmental pollution and the oil industry in the Niger Delta (much of it led by Shell International).

Michael Jacobs on sustainable development

Governments often speak of aiming for 'sustainable growth'; they mean economic growth without inflation rather than without environmental degradation, and the usual interpretation of 'sustainable' is lasting about four years, or until the next election, whichever is the sooner. (Jacobs, 1993: 9)

It needs to be remembered after all that sustainable development and sustainability were not originally intended as 'economic' terms. They were, and remain, essentially ethico-political objectives, more like 'social justice' and 'democracy' than 'economic growth'. And as such, their purpose or 'use' is mainly to express key ideas about how society – including the economy – should be governed. (Jacobs, 1995: 65)

Figure 13.2 Swampy protesting over Manchester Airport, 1997.

neat word, sustainability hides a theoretical maze of great complexity (Daly, 1990; Lélé, 1991). It offers a verbal flourish, but at its core is a theoretical black hole (Redclift, 1984, 1987).

Of course, it is not strictly fair to say that sustainability has no theoretical core. Its intellectual roots lie in population biology, ecology and economics. Through the 1920s and 1930s, biologists were developing simple mathematical models of population growth and competition, from which, in time, grew the notion of maximum sustainable yield, that populations of organisms (initially fish, but the point was generally true) could be harvested at a rate that allowed the population to reproduce itself.

These scientific ideas about how animal populations fluctuated, and what happens when people start to harvest them, comprise one stream of biological ideas feeding into sustainability. A second is in ecology, particularly in the concept of the ecosystem (proposed in the 1930s), and in ideas about plant succession. As ecology became influenced by systems thinking in the 1960s, ideas of equilibrium in ecosystems provided a further natural science basis for ideas of sustainability. The science of ecology seemed to show the vulnerability of the environment to human impacts, and the need for those impacts to be moderated. Meanwhile, from economics came concepts of renewable (flow) and non-renewable (stock) resources. These are diverse enough roots, but onto them many other ideas were grafted from the emerging world view of environmentalism, particularly about population growth, resource exhaustion and the toxic and shocking effects of industrialization and urbanization (Adams, 1990).

Summary

Sustainability tends to be defined in different ways by different interests, for example, by environmental organizations and big business.

The concept of sustainability draws on specific studies of the dynamics of animal populations and ecosystem equilibrium, and ideas about the economics of renewable resource exploitation.

SUSTAINABILITY AND THIRD WORLD DEVELOPMENT

The concept of sustainability first emerged at the United Nations Conference on the Human Environment, held at Stockholm in 1972 (Adams, 1990; McCormick, 1992). This meeting was the direct forerunner of the Rio Conference 20 years later. Like Rio, it saw profound divisions between industrialized countries and the Third World. The poorer non-aligned countries saw the First World's concerns about pollution and technology as the worries of an exclusive club of wealthy countries, and a potential threat to their ability to industrialize effectively. They also feared and resented the obsession of environmentalists in the First World with population growth (see Box page 118). The concept of sustainable development was coined explicitly to argue that an option existed that would allow appropriate (ie rapid) economic growth and industrialization without environmental damage. This happy outcome has been the target of all subsequent calls for sustainability.

Since Stockholm, different interests have emphasized different aspects of sustainability, and sought to claim the concept for their own. In 1980 the World Conservation Strategy (IUCN, 1980) took a strongly conservation-oriented position. It defined conservation as sustained resource use, and suggested three objectives for global conservation. The objectives of the World Conservation Strategy are:

- to maintain essential ecological processes and life support systems (such as soil regeneration and protection, the recycling of nutrients, and the cleansing of waters);
- to preserve genetic diversity (the range of genetic material found in the world's organisms);
- to ensure the sustainable utilization of species and ecosystems (notably fish and other wildlife, forests and grazing lands).

Six years later, the report of the World Commission on Environment and Development, *Our Common Future* (called the Brundtland Report after its Chair), had a very different emphasis. It deliberately broadened the debate, locating environmental issues within the economic and political context of international development debates. It therefore linked basic development needs and environmental degradation, arguing that one could not be solved without the other. The way forward, it suggested, was through global multilateral co-operation between rich and poor countries to achieve development: sustainability achieved through careful economic growth.

The Brundtland Report, published in 1986, led directly to UNCED, in two ways. First, it was debate of the report in the General Assembly of the UN that led to the resolution to hold what became the Rio Conference. Second, it was this message of adapted or 'green' growth that provided the carrot to persuade both rich and poor countries to come to the negotiating table. None the less, the task of finding common ground was Herculean, and lasted through a full five years of preparatory meetings before the conference itself (Chatterjee and Finger, 1994). The documents produced by this 'Rio process' were the fruit of wearying debate far into the night by government delegations determined to produce a form of words that gave least away in terms of their own national interests.

Inevitably, divisions opened up over the distinction between countries in the industrialized 'North' and the underdeveloped 'South'. They disagreed over what the main global problems were (global atmospheric change, biodiversity loss and tropical deforestation in the industrialized countries, poverty and the environmental problems associated with it in unindustrialized countries), and they disagreed over who should pay for any action needed. Third World countries feared that their development would be stifled by restrictive international agreements on atmospheric emissions (just as at Stockholm in 1972), and they were jealous of their right to use the natural resources within their boundaries for development (notably tropical forests) without restriction by environmentalists in the First World (whose environmental concerns, arguably, were only possible because of wealth itself created by polluting freely and consuming forests and other resources).

Eventually, some kind of agreement was patched together, and the conference agreed a slightly rambling set of 29 principles in the 'Rio Declaration', a much watered-down set of principles for forest management (unexcitingly titled a 'Non Legally Binding Authoritative Statement of Principles for a Global Consensus on the Management, Conservation and Sustainable Development of all Types of Forests'), and the vast compendium of good intentions in Agenda 21. Samuel Johnson, the essayist and first compiler of an English dictionary, is said to have

apologized for the length of a letter, saying 'I did not have time to make it short'. So it was with Agenda 21, which contains more than 600 pages of text in 40 separate chapters. These were divided into four sections, covering socio-economic and environmental aspects of sustainable development, the actors who could make it happen, and the means of implementation (see Box page 119).

Agenda 21 has become an icon of sustainable development worshipped but not much read. Because of the way it was written through negotiation, every commitment has a get-out clause somewhere nearby. It contains therefore within it most possible arguments, and is readily mined for nuggets of text that can be

used to legitimatize any given point of view.

However, the Rio Conference was a watershed. From then on, governments and international agencies began to re-interpret their normal work of economic planning within the new, internationally agreed, terminology. There was a substantial shift in political and bureaucratic rhetoric, but the new language sometimes lay wafer-thin across old and not obviously 'sustainable' policies. A shift in the language of policy of this magnitude, of course, is no small matter. It was due to two related forces. First, it was a straight-forward response by politicians (particularly in Europe and North America) to the surge of environmentalism that took place

Population, environment and sustainability

In the 1970s, First World environmentalists laid particular emphasis on the problem of population growth, arguing that as populations rose resource exploitation would inevitably become unsustainable. This argument was particularly made about rural populations in the Third World. Books like *The Population Bomb* by Paul Ehrlich (1972), and papers like Garret Hardin's 'The tragedy of the commons' (published in *Science* in 1968), started a new and apocalyptic 'neo-Malthusian' debate about people and environment. Through the 1970s and 1980s, the drylands of Sub-Saharan Africa were singled out in particular as a place where rapid population growth was leading to environmental degradation. Drought and famine were both significant problems in this decade, but attention focused in particular on the problem of 'desertification' and human-made deserts. It was widely held (not least by geographers) that population growth inevitably led to desertification, as farmers and pastoralists pushed semi-arid ecosystems past some natural limit.

However, research in recent years has begun to show that in several parts of Africa

agricultural systems appear to have coped with significant levels of population growth without loss of sustainability. The most important study of this kind was conducted in the Machakos District in Kenya (Tiffen et al., 1994). In the 1930s, government officials despaired of Machakos, which was thought to be on the verge of ecological collapse due to over-population. Fifty years later, the changes have been remarkable. The population has soared (from 0.24m in 1930 to 1.4m in 1990), but far from destroying the environment, farmers have developed it. Terracing is extensive, cattle are stall-fed and their manure applied to the land (see Figs 13.4 and 13.5), and with the advent of cash crops (particularly coffee), the volume and value of output have increased to match population growth. It is an astonishing story, and while the experience of this area might not be a good model for the whole of Africa (among other things, the international city of Nairobi is not far from the borders of Machakos, and the main road to the coast passes through it), it is clearly unwise to make the automatic assumption that rural population growth is unsustainable.

The contents of Agenda 21

Section 1
Social and Economic Dimensions: Eight chapters, covering international co-operation, combating poverty, consumption
5 patterns, population, health settlements and integrated environment and development decision-making.

Section 2
Conservation and Management of
10 **Resources for Development:** Fourteen chapters on the environment. These covered the atmosphere, oceans, freshwaters and water resources, land resource management, deforestation, desertification, mountain
15 environments, sustainable agriculture and rural development. They also covered the conservation of biological diversity and biotechnology, toxic, hazardous, solid and radioactive wastes.

20 ### Section 3
Strengthening the Role of Major Groups: Ten chapters discussing the role of women, young people and indigenous people in sustainable development; the role of non-
25 governmental organizations, local authorities, trade unions, business and scientists and farmers.

Section 4
Means of Implementation: Eight chapters,
30 exploring how to pay for sustainable development, the need to transfer environmentally sound technology and science; the role of education, international capacity-building; international legal
35 instruments and information flow.

(Robinson, 1993)

480 within Western societies in the early 1990s. Behind that pragmatic (perhaps sometimes cynical) politics lay a perception of environmental limits, which
485 had itself driven that rise of environmental concern. As Bill McKibben wrote in his best-selling book *The End of Nature*, 'The greenhouse effect is the
490 first environmental problem we can't escape by moving to the woods' (McKibben, 1990: 188). Sustainability and sustainable development were the words
495 people in the 1990s came to use to express that thought, and on which they tried to build arguments for reform.

Figure 13.3 Smoke plume from UK power station: concern about acid rain was one of the environmental problems that led to the Stockholm Conference.

Figure 13.4 Terraced farmland in Machakos.

Figure 13.5 Stall-fed cows, Machakos.

Source: Adams, W.M. (1999) 'Sustainability' in Cloke P. et al (eds) *Introducing Human Geographies* London: Arnold, pp. 125–129

SUSTAINABLE
URBAN LIVELIHOODS

- Jobless growth in cities of the developing world

- The nature of the Brown Agenda

- Ecological footprints and the regional impacts of cities

- The capacity and effectiveness of city authorities as core conditions for sustainable urban development

- Enabling social organization at the local level

Introduction

The proportion of people living in urban areas of the globe is increasing, and particularly in the developing world. Whilst in 1800, only 3 per cent of the total world population lived in towns and cities, it is estimated that by the year 2000, this figure will have risen to over 50 per cent (United Nations, 1989). Although a greater
5 proportion of the population of the developed world currently live in cities, as seen in Figure 5.1 (approximately 73 per cent or 900 million people), the total size of the urban population is larger in the developing world, at around 1,400 million people, as seen in Figure 5.2 (Devas and Rakodi, 1993). In addition 93 per cent of the predicted urban growth to the year 2020 will occur in the developing world.

10 In 1987, the World Commission on Environment and Development suggested that the urban challenge lay 'firmly in the developing countries' (WCED, 1987: 237), due in the main to the unprecedented growth rates, but also to the challenge of meeting the current needs of an expanding urban poor. In that year, for example, the World Bank had estimated that approximately one-quarter of the developing world's absolute
15 poor were living in urban areas (World Bank, 1990a). By the turn of the century, this figure is expected to be nearer 50 per cent, as highlighted in Chapter 2.

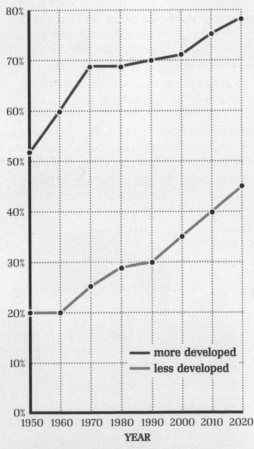

Figure 5.1 *The proportion of the population expected to be living in urban areas.* Source: UN (1989)

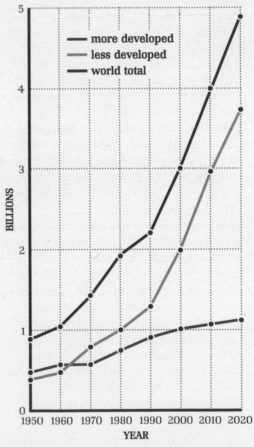

Figure 5.2 *Projected population living in urban areas.* Source: UN (1989)

Cities are central to attempts at meeting the goals of sustainable development in the sense that this is where the majority of the world's population will soon be located, with all the associated physical demands (such as for food and shelter) and the political, social and
20 cultural requirements associated with the adoption of urban values. In addition, city-based production currently accounts for the majority of resource consumption and waste generation world-wide (WRI, 1996). Throughout history, cities have been a driving force in development processes and, as cities grow, productive activities tend to concentrate in urban centres. For example, an estimated 80 per cent of GDP growth in the developing
25 world in the 1990s originates in cities and towns (Bartone *et al.,* 1994). Wealthier cities, and higher income groups within urban areas, consume the highest levels of resources and contribute disproportionately to waste generation (WRI, 1996).

There are substantial challenges for *all* cities in managing the environmental implications of economic growth, in meeting the needs of their residents and for protecting the
30 environmental resources on which they depend into the future. The focus of this chapter is the particular challenges of cities in the developing world, where it will be seen that the unprecedented rates of urban growth and industrialisation in combination with poverty create distinct and immediate environmental problems which to a large extent are not key concerns in wealthier cities. Figure 5.3 depicts a general characterisation of how
35 environmental problems and the severity of their impacts differ within cities at various levels of income. The 'pollution' of urban poverty that arises from inadequate water supplies, sanitation, drainage and solid waste collection is seen to be the most immediate problem of cities in the developing world. These issues have been termed the 'Brown Agenda'. In wealthier cities, the key challenges for action lie in reducing excessive
40 consumption of natural resources and the burden of wastes on the global environment (WRI, 1996). This 'Green Agenda', encompassing the depletion of water and forest resources, for example, has tended to receive greater international attention, because of the relation to issues of global environmental change such as climate warming.

However, such typologies or distinctions should not distort the common, global challenges
45 of sustainable urban development. Whilst the Brown Agenda is the priority for low-income countries, actions are also needed in the cities of the developing world to promote the efficient use of resources and the minimisation of waste, if they are to prosper in future without the ecological impact of past developments as currently evidenced in 'first world' cities. In addition, as emphasised throughout earlier chapters, processes of
50 globalisation are producing a far more integrated and interdependent world economy into the 1990s. Cities across the globe are experiencing change, not solely in terms of their size, but also in respect of the activities they host and the function they play in the world's
55 economic, trading and political systems (Hamnett, 1995). This chapter details the primary characteristics of these processes of change and patterns of urban development in the developing world in order to understand
60 more fully the specific nature of the challenges and opportunities of sustainable development in this sector.

Figure 5.3 *Economic-environmental typology of cities*

Urban environmental problems	Lower-income countries (<$650/cap)	Lower- to middle-income countries ($660 – 2,500/cap)	Upper- to middle-income countries ($2,500 – 6,500/cap)	Upper-income countries (>$6,500/cap)
ACCESS TO BASIC SERVICES				
Water supply and sanitation	Low coverage and poor quality, especially for urban poor	Low access for urban poor	Generally acceptable water supply, reasonable sewerage	Good; concern with trace substances
Drainage	Low coverage: frequent flooding	Inadequate; frequent flooding	Reasonable	Good
Solid waste collection	Low coverage: especially for urban poor	Inadequate	Reasonable	Good
POLLUTION				
Water pollution	Problems from inadequate sanitation and raw domestic sewage	Severe problems from untreated municipal discharges	Severe problems from poorly treated municipal and industrial discharges	High levels of treatment; concern with amenity values and toxic substances
Air pollution	Severe problems in some cities using soft coal; indoor exposure for poor	Severe problems in many cities from soft coal use and/or vehicle emissions	Severe problems in many cities from soft coal use and/or vehicle emissions	Problems in some cities from vehicle emissions; health priority
Solid waste disposal	Open dumping, mixed wastes	Mostly uncontrolled landfills, mixed wastes	Semi-controlled landfills	Controlled landfills, incineration, resource recovery
Hazardous waste management	Non-existent capacity	Severe problems, little capacity	Severe problems, growing capacity	Moving from remediation to prevention
RESOURCE LOSSES				
Land management	Uncontrolled land development and use; pressure from squatter settlements	Ineffective land use controls	Some environmental zoning practised	Environmental zoning commonplace
ENVIRONMENTAL HAZARDS				
Natural and man-made hazards	Recurrent disasters with severe damage and loss of life	Recurrent disasters with damage and loss of life	High risk from industrial disasters	Good emergency response capacity

Source: Bartone et al. (1994)

Urban change in the developing world

Patterns

Whilst the general trend across the developing world, as seen in Figures 5.1 and 5.2, is
65 for increasing levels of urbanisation, there are significant differences between regions
and countries in the patterns of change. For example, it can be seen in Table 5.1 that the
highest growth rates to date have been in Africa which is also where the most rapid
change in the near future is predicted to occur. However, it is in South and South-East
Asia that the largest numbers of people currently reside in urban areas and where the
70 greatest future expansion in terms of additional urban residents will occur. Countries
such as India have very large urban (as well as total) populations, for example. Indian
cities such as Calcutta and Bombay are amongst the largest centres in Asia (as seen in
Figure 5.4) and indeed the world (see Figure 5.5). It should be noted, however, that for
some of the largest cities in the developing world, growth rates during the 1980s were
75 significantly slower than during the 1960s and 1970s (UNCHS, 1996).

In many developing countries, a high proportion of the urban population is concentrated
in one or two major cities. This pattern is more established in the countries of Latin
America than in any other developing region (Hardoy and Satterthwaite, 1989). By 1985,
for example, Mexico City, São Paulo, Buenos Aires, and Rio de Janeiro all had populations
80 in excess of 10 million. In contrast, there were no cities of this size in the whole African
continent by this date (although Cairo came close). In short, Africa's contemporary rapid
urban growth rates are occurring over a relatively small base and are more widely
distributed across many smaller and intermediate urban centres. Indeed, the 'explosive
growth' of mega-cities in the developing world which was predicted in the early 1980s
85 has not generally been realised. Although there is a growing number of urban centres of
unprecedented size, something under 5 per cent of the global population live in mega-
cities (UNCHS, 1996). New kinds of urban systems are also developing world-wide which
include networks of very dynamic, although smaller cities (see Potter *et al.,* 1999). In short,
the actual and predicted patterns of urban change in the developing world have been the
90 subject of much analysis and debate and have proved to be highly varied even within
nations and not always as expected by researchers or planners.

Processes

The key processes of urban change in the developing world are certainly without historical
precedent. In nineteenth-century Europe, people migrated to the towns and cities in search
95 of employment and economic advancement. The industrial activities located in those areas
depended on this process of migration to raise output, and generate wealth. Urbanisation,
industrialisation and 'modernisation' (the adoption of urban values) were processes
which occurred simultaneously in the cities of Europe, and were mutually reinforcing. This
has not been the case in the developing world. Table 5.2 highlights the cases of a number of
100 Latin American countries in the 1960s (a period of relatively rapid industrial development),
where it is seen that employment growth lagged substantially behind that in manufacturing
output. Such 'jobless growth' continued to be a feature of urban change in the developing
world into the 1990s.

Table 5.1 *Urban population change by region, 1970–2000*

	Urban population, 1985 (millions)	Urban population, growth rate, 1970–85 (per cent)	Projected urban population, 2000 (millions)	Projected urban population growth rate, 1985–2000 (per cent)
China	219	1.8	322	2.6
East Asia	46	4.4	68	2.6
South and South-East Asia	377	4.1	694	4.2
West Asia	63	4.6	109	3.7
Latin America	279	3.6	417	2.7
Africa	174	5.0	361	5.0
Pacific	1	4.2	2	4.7
Total	1,159	3.7	1,972	3.6

Source: Devas and Rakodi (1993)

Table 5.2 *Industrialisation and employment in selected Latin American countries, 1963–9*

Country	Manufacturing annual output growth (%)	Manufacturing employment growth (%)
Brazil	6.5	1.1
Colombia	5.9	2.8
Costa Rica	8.9	2.8
Dominican Republic	1.7	-3.3
Ecuador	11.4	6.0
Panama	12.9	7.4

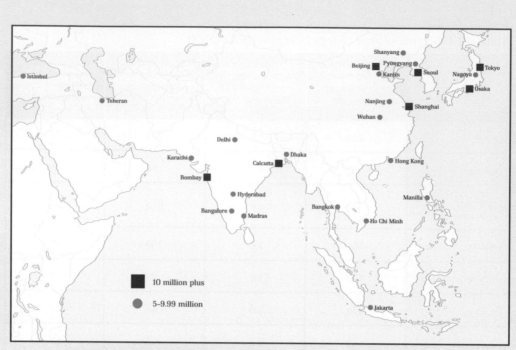

Figure 5.4 *The largest urban centres in Asia*
Source: UNCHS (1996)

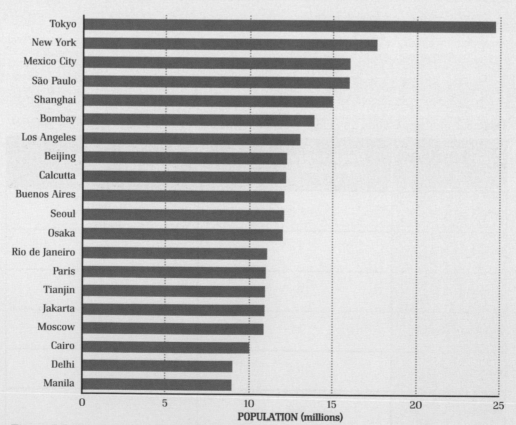

Figure 5.5 *The world's largest urban agglomerations in 1990*
Source: UNCHS (1996)

Few of the urban poor can afford to be unemployed for any length of time. Many, in
105 fact, will be under-employed; either they are working less than they would like or are
doing so at such low rates of production that their labour could be withdrawn with
very little impact on overall output. In recent years, structural adjustment programmes
have also led to contraction in formal sector employment opportunities in the cities of
the developing world, through the loss of jobs in the public sector and the
110 denationalisation of industries, for example. In response to a lack of employment
opportunities within this 'formal' sector, many urban residents in the developing
world look to a wide variety of both legitimate and illegitimate income opportunities
available within the 'informal' economy, the term used to refer commonly to small-
scale, unregulated, semi-legal economic activities which often rely on indigenous
115 resources, family labour and traditional technology. Whilst it is now appreciated that
the two sectors are not wholly distinct (see Drakakis-Smith, 1987), Table 5.3 shows the
estimated share of urban labour force in the informal sector for a number of cities in
the developing world. Clearly, in urban areas employment is critical to securing a
livelihood and avoiding impoverishment and for sustained development. Todaro (1997)
120 has suggested that one of the most 'obvious failures' of the development process
over the past few decades has been 'the failure of modern urban industries to
generate a significant number of employment opportunities' (p. 247).

Source: Elliot J.A. (1999) *An Introduction to Sustainable Development*, London: Routledge

TRANSPORT:

REDUCING AUTOMOBILE DEPENDENCE

SUMMARY: SUCCESSFUL AND WEALTHY CITIES ARE USUALLY ASSOCIATED WITH HIGH LEVELS OF AUTOMOBILE USE AND ARE STRUGGLING TO COPE WITH THE LARGE ECONOMIC, SOCIAL AND ENVIRONMENTAL COSTS THIS BRINGS. THIS PAPER
5 SHOWS HOW SUCH CITIES DO NOT NEED TO DEPEND ON HIGH LEVELS OF PRIVATE AUTOMOBILE USE AND DESCRIBES HOW AUTOMOBILE .DEPENDENCE HAS BEEN REDUCED IN MANY OF THE MOST SUCCESSFUL CITIES IN THE NORTH AND KEPT RELATIVELY LOW IN SOME OF THE WEALTHIEST CITIES
10 IN THE SOUTH.

INTRODUCTION

In the post-war era falling energy prices and rising car ownership have transformed cities, allowing the increased physical separation of activities and the progressive spread of urban hinterland at lower densities. The dispersal of employment, retailing and service facilities creates an equivalently dispersed pattern of trips that is anathema to public transport operation. Lower average densities mean a decline in pedestrian accessibility, longer trip lengths and reduced catchment populations for public transport routes. The result is increased car dependence, profligate energy use and global pollution.

The extent to which a city's population has become dependent on the use of private automobiles varies greatly, even for cities where the inhabitants have comparable levels of income. A detailed study of 32 major cities in North America, Europe, Australia and Asia found that the cities could be divided into five categories of automobile dependence. Most US and Australian cities were within categories one and two which have a high or very high automobile dependence and, at most, a minor role for public transport, walking and cycling. Most European cities fell into categories three and four that had moderate or low automobile dependence and an important role for public transport. However, Munich and Paris, both among the most prosperous cities in Europe, along with three of the most prosperous Asian cities (Tokyo, Singapore, Hong Kong) had a very low automobile dependence with public transport, walking and cycling more important than cars.

TRENDS IN AUTOMOBILE DEPENDENCE

The global cities study mentioned earlier is being updated to include data for 1990. The 1980s was the first decade where it would be possible to judge the impact of the global sustainability agenda on cities in terms of their transportation. The early data are summarized in Table 8.2, showing trends.

CAR USE TRENDS

US cities have continued to accelerate in car use per capita (2.3 per cent in the 1980s compared to 2.2 per cent in the 1970s); their 2,400 kilometres of growth per capita in the ten years to 1990 is equal to the total vehicle kilometres travelled (VKT) per capita in Paris or London in the 1980s. European and Asian cities starting from a much lower base grew only 950 kilometres and 420 kilometres per capita, though this 2.2 per cent and 3.3 per cent per annum growth is still a real concern for a sustainable future.

Australian and Canadian cities are showing an interesting trend towards reduced growth in VKT. In the 1960s, Australian cities' VKT grew by 4.5 per cent, by 2.3 per cent in the 1970s and by 1.2 per cent in the 1980s. If projected, this leads to zero growth in the 1990s (see Figure 8.3).

Toronto is similar (along with other Canadian cities in preliminary data) with just 1.6 per cent growth in the 1980s (873 kilometres of growth per capita). Figure 8.4 shows the differences between the US and other cities in terms of the growth in vehicle kilometres travelled in cars per person during the 1980s.

The reduced growth in car use in Australian and Canadian cities (especially compared to US cities) may be due to:

- Reurbanization of older suburbs which leads to reduced travel: reurbanization in Australian cities is now more than 30 per cent and up to 50 per cent of all development; it is also very strong in Canadian cities.

- Development of nodal subcentres in outer suburbs that also reduce the need for travel and make transit more viable; signs of these emerging subcentres are apparent in Australia but not as much as in Canadian cities.

- Better urban environments which encourage both the reduction in the need for car journeys to 'leapfrog' unsafe urban areas (as in US cities), and more walking and cycling.

- Less dispersion and development of highly car-dependent 'edge cities' which have been characteristic of US urban growth patterns.

Table 8.2 *Trends in the use per person of automobiles and public transport in world cities, by region*

Car use (vehicle kilometres travelled per person)			
Year	1970	1980	1990
US cities	7,334	9,168	11,559
Australian cities	4,628	5,850	6,589
Toronto	n/a	4,807	5,680
European cities	2,750	3,798	4,754
Asian cities	913	1,067	1,487

Public transportation (trips per person)			
Year	1970	1980	1990
US cities	48	57	64
Australian cities	118	93	91
Toronto	154	202	210
European cities	249	290	359
Asian cities	454	430	496

Sources: ESCAP. *State of Urbanization in Asia and the Pacific 1993,* Economic and Social Commission for Asia and the Pacific, ST/ESCAP/1300. United Nations, New York, 1993; Kenworthy, Jeff. Paul Barter, Peter Newman and Chamlong Poboon (1994), 'Resisting automobile dependence in booming economies; a case study of Singapore, Tokyo and Hong Kong within a global sample of cities', paper presented at the Asian Studies Association of Australia Biennial Conference, 1994. Murdoch University, Perth; and Urban Redevelopment Authority (1991), *Living the Next Lap: Towards a Tropical City of Excellence,* Singapore.

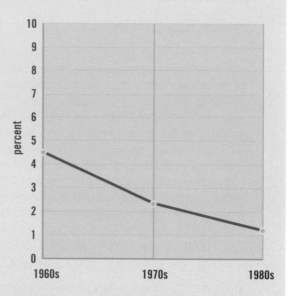

Figure 8.3 *Average increase in car use (vehicle kilometres travelled per capita) in Australian cities*

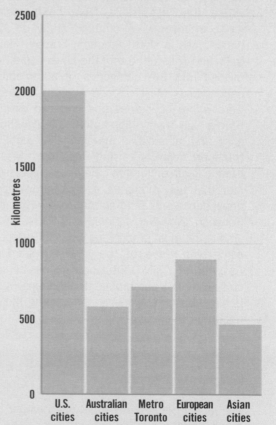

Figure 8.4 *Increases in car use (vehicle kilometres travelled per capita) in global cities, 1980–1990*

PUBLIC TRANSPORT USE

Despite predictions by Lave that transit can never compete with the car and that it is in a terminal state of decline every-
110 where, the actual data from most cities is quite positive (see Figure 8.5).

Transit in US cities is still low but is growing again. In Australian cities it has stabilized and indeed may have started growing again in
115 the 1990s. It grew in Toronto, the European cities and the Asian cities. The average transit trips per capita growth in European cities is more than the total per capita use in US cities. In Asian cities the growth was
120 much more again. Growth in transit in European cities is accelerating (2.1 per cent in the 1980s compared to 1.5 per cent in the 1970s). Such trends are a positive sign of sustainability.

125 Some of the world's wealthiest and most successful cities have been reducing their citizens' dependence on private automobiles. This can be seen in a comparison between Los Angeles, Zurich and Singapore
130 on how their car use and transit use changed between 1980 and 1990. In Los Angeles, car use continued to grow rapidly, with a decline in the use of public transit, whereas in Zurich and Singapore there was
135 far less growth in car use and a considerable increase in the use of public transit. Thus, the substantial increases in income which have occurred in the past ten years in Zurich and Singapore have gone mostly into public
140 transit use and not into private car use and this reflects their cities' overall plans and priorities to achieve this. Los Angeles, on the other hand, has not attempted to control automobile dependence; here, it is
145 accepted that there is a culture which has little belief in planning other than the facilitation of individual mobility. The use of private automobiles has almost inevitably grown as a result.

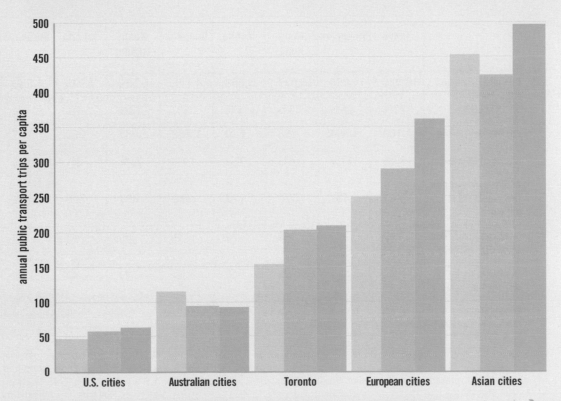

Figure 8.5 *Trends in per capita public transport use in world cities by region, 1970–1990*

THE ASIAN CITIES STUDY

We are conducting a more detailed study of the sustainability of seven Asian cities. This is being done partly for the World Bank to highlight further the question of transportation priorities and their link to land use and infrastructure as well as the role of personal income in shaping these patterns. Table 8.3 contains the preliminary data. The data indicate the following:

There is little obvious relationship between automobile travel patterns and income. Hong Kong, Singapore and Tokyo average 13 per cent of the car use of US cities despite having much higher wealth levels (average of 44 per cent, with Tokyo being 77 per cent of US cities). Their wealth is much more directed into transit, which is on average eight times US levels. Bangkok, Kuala Lumpur, Jakarta and Surabaya have only 10 per cent of US incomes and are thus much poorer than Tokyo, Singapore and Hong Kong. On the other hand, transit use is generally underdeveloped compared to the richer Asian cities (about half of Manila is not considered – see below). These are the cities (especially Bangkok) where traffic levels are major economic and environmental issues. Thus, it appears that their wealth is being converted into automobile use on the American model in these cities rather than into transit as found in the Singapore, Tokyo and Hong Kong model. Manila has a very high transit use with its Jitney system, though its 727 trips per capita is not as impressive when compared on a passenger / kilometre basis, as most trips are very short. As car use grows it is increasingly difficult for transit to remain competitive, thus Manila is preparing to build more segregated electric rail services.

Table 8.3 *Transportation infrastructure and land use in seven Asian cities, 1990.*

	Tokyo	Singapore	Hong Kong	Manila	Bangkok	Kuala Lumpur	Jakarta	Surabaya
City median income (US$ 1990) and % of US	38,229 77%	12,860 26%	15,077 30%	3,058 6%	4,132 8%	6,539 13%	1,975 4%	1,975 4%
Car use per person (km) and % of US car use	2,103 19%	1,864 17%	493 4%	860 8%	1,562 14%	2,687 24%	383 3%	237 2%
Public transport use per capita (trips per year)	461	457	570	727	340	337	206	122
% of motorized trips by public transport	62	72	89	73	31	30	47	29
% of all trips by walking and cycling	45	n/a	n/a	30	14	20	43	25
Length of road (metres per person)	19	1.0	0.3	0.6	0.6	1.5	0.5	0.3

Source: Kenworthy, Jeff; Paul Barter; Peter Newman and Chamlong Poboon (1994), 'Resisting automobile dependence in booming economies: a case study of Singapore, Tokyo and Hong Kong within a global sample of cities', paper presented at the Asian Studies Association of Australia Biennial Conference 1994, Murdoch University, Perth; and Urban Redevelopment Authority (1991), *Living the Next Lap: Towards a Tropical City of Excellence*, Singapore

190 Jakarta and Surabaya have comparatively very little car use but also the lowest level of transit use. Traffic issues are generally leading to higher automobile infrastructure rather than to more transit. These Indonesian 195 cities are faced with a future like Bangkok's if they continue down that path.

- In peak periods, when road space is at a premium, cities such as Tokyo, Hong Kong, Singapore and Manila average 74 per cent of 200 motorized work trips on transit. On the other hand, Bangkok, Kuala Lumpur and Surabaya have a mere 30 per cent, highlighting a growing difference in transportation priorities in these cities. Jakarta is between these two 205 groups with 47 per cent.

- Modal split patterns also vary in interesting ways. Wealthy Tokyo has a very large 45 per cent of all trips on foot and by bicycle, while much poorer Bangkok and Kuala Lumpur have 210 only 14 per cent and 20 per cent respectively. Traffic in Bangkok is now so bad it makes any walking or cycling almost impossible. Private transportation accounts for over 50 per cent of total trips in Bangkok and Kuala Lumpur, while 215 in Tokyo it is only 27 per cent. In Surabaya, the least wealthy of all the cities, 47 per cent of trips are now by private transportation (particularly motorcycles) and walking and cycling has fallen to 35 per cent, down from 53 per 220 cent in 1980.

- All these Asian cities have land-use structures that are built for transit and walking rather than for automobiles. Those cities opting to facilitate automobile use rather than transit are 225 showing all the signs of an inherently dysfunctional system. They also have a much better chance of coping with a world where automobile dependence must be overcome (including the sustainability agenda to reduce fuel use 230 and greenhouse gas production) than US and Australian cities. They just need to invest in the transit/cycling/walking infrastructure. US and Australian cities must also restructure their urban form.

235 SOLUTIONS TO AUTOMOBILE DEPENDENCE

National and city governments in both the North and the South are questioning the future of cities and urban systems in which 240 private automobiles have the central role in the transport of people. This stems from a greater recognition of the economic, social and environmental costs of 'automobile-dependent' cities that were described 245 above. Solutions to automobile dependence are thus being sought across the globe.

Automobiles and trucks can be 'civilized' through technological advances that greatly reduce fuel use and polluting emissions 250 and increase safety both for the vehicle users and for other road users. Sophisticated traffic management systems can increase efficiency in the use of road spaces and the number of vehicles using 255 road systems without congestion. But, increasingly, even if the incorporation of these advances was accelerated, it is seen as insufficient as the sheer volume of cars, trucks and other motorized road vehicles 260 overwhelms cities. This is especially so in high-density cities that have a low proportion of their total area devoted to roads, as in many cities in Europe and in the South. Seeking to expand road systems to cope 265 with projections of increased automobile use in high-density cities also disrupts the urban fabric and displaces large numbers of people. It was the scale of this disruption in cities in the North that helped to 270 generate a re-evaluation of the priority that was being given to private automobile users. For many of the major cities in the South, the number of automobiles is growing much more rapidly than the 275 number of people, and building the roads and highways to cope with projections for increased automobile use will mean the displacement of tens of thousands (or more) people in each such city. There 280 is also the more recent recognition that people who do not have access to a car are significantly disadvantaged as automobile dependence within a city or region increases since this also leads to a deterioration in 285 public transit and a city in which access to workplaces, schools, shops and services is increasingly difficult without a car.

Despite the doubts as to whether the use of private cars can be controlled, not least 290 because of the power of the economic interests behind the automobile-dependent model, there is a growing awareness of the need to plan to reduce automobile-dependence within cities. Many cities have pedestri- 295 anized their central districts; for most, this was easily done as these were historic city centres that originally developed as 'walking cities' before the advent of motorized transport. But there are also many examples 300 of cities which have reduced automobile dependence through innovations in public transit and controls on automobile use in both the North and the South. They include Hong Kong, Singapore and Surabaya in 305 Asia, Curitiba in Latin America, Zurich, Copenhagen and Freiburg in Europe, Toronto and Portland in North America and Perth in Australia, and the means by which they achieved this are outlined below. The fact 310 that this list includes some of the wealthiest cities in both the North and South shows that reducing automobile dependence is possible even in societies with high levels of automobile ownership.

315 There is also much discussion about the need for public transit-oriented development as the basis for any sustainable city. The link with sustainable development comes from the fact that there is a rapid growth in the 320 number of automobile-dependent cities and in most of these cities, automobile depend-ence is still increasing. The world's con-sumption of fossil fuels and total emissions of greenhouse gases would 325 increase dramatically if the whole world's population came to be as automobile dependent as North America, Western

Europe or Australia. The OECD and the World Bank have begun to recognize this and 330 are stressing how transport funding needs to be more critically evaluated. But, in a globally connected world, the reduction of automobile dependence (and its associated energy use, resource use, air pollution and 335 greenhouse gas emissions) should be directed both to cities where automobile dependence is highest and to cities in the South where short-term and long-term measures can reduce their automobile 340 dependence while also enhancing their prosperity and quality of life.

KEY POLICY CONCLUSIONS

Four key conclusions of relevance to public policy can be drawn from the data 345 on cities around the world as to how auto-mobile dependence can be reduced:

- *Public transport infrastructure* – investment in transit infrastructure can help to shape the city as well as ease traffic problems – for instance, 350 encouraging 'walking cities' to develop around light railway or rapid busway stations. There is a considerable range of technological options too, varying in price, capacity and speed and these include options such as express busways 355 that do not require heavy investments. It is also possible to 'upgrade' as demand rises and as cities grow in size and wealth – for instance, as light railways or trams replace express busways. It is also possible to draw on private 360 sector resources – for instance, through city authorities providing the framework within which private bus companies bid for particular routes or areas. But this can only be achieved if public transit is part of a broader policy that 365 discourages low-density developments and unnecessary automobile use. If public transit is left as a supplementary process in streets designed for the automobile, there will be no resolution of the transport dilemma.

370 • *Pedestrian/cycle orientation* – if the goal is to provide for the most efficient, equitable and human form of transport, this means a city with provision for cycling, good walking space on streets and in public squares, and traffic-free
375 shopping streets. Any city that neglects this dimension will find social and economic problems as well as the obvious environmental ones.

• *Density* – the need to maintain land-use efficiency is linked closely to transport. Dispersing
380 land uses at low density creates automobile dependence. Dense urban villages linked by public transit creates the opportunity for 'walking city' and 'transit city' characteristics to be introduced into the automobile-dependent
385 city (see Figure 8.5, which should be compared to Figure 8.2). Similarly, introducing new and efficient public transit lines into rapidly growing cities can encourage the development of such dense urban settlements and limit
390 low-density sprawl, especially if land-use planning helps to encourage such developments.

• *Planning and control* – all three of the above policies have strong market pressures behind them. But they also require planning to facilitate
395 them. This planning is not heavy-handed bureaucracy but an expression of any city's cultural values, and also of the needs and priorities of pedestrians and cyclists and of children, youth and all other citizens who
400 cannot or do not use cars. All cities have some commitment to this social value. If automobile dependence is not resisted through conscious planning, it will erode or help to destroy most attempts to maintain community life in an urban
405 setting. For all cities, but particularly those in the South, strong neighbourhoods need to be protected from the dispersing and disruptive aspects of the automobile, while in many cities in the wealthiest market economies of the
410 world, the policy of reducing automobile dependence is part of a process to reclaim residential neighbourhoods.

Source: Newman, P. (1999) 'Transport: Reducing Automobile Dependence' in Satterthwaite, D. (ed.) *The Earthscan reader in Sustainable Cities*, London: Earthscan Publications.

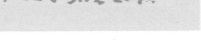

APPENDIX 5: Compiling a bibliography

A book – single author

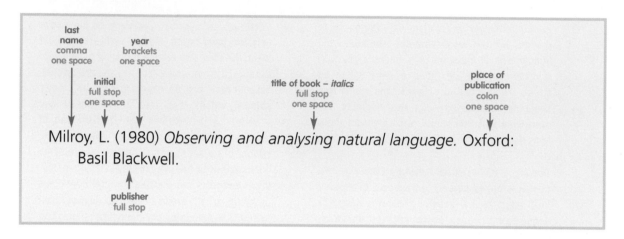

A book – more than one author

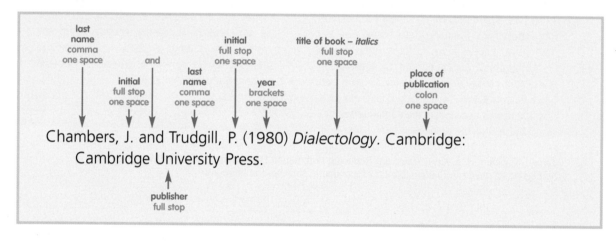

A journal article

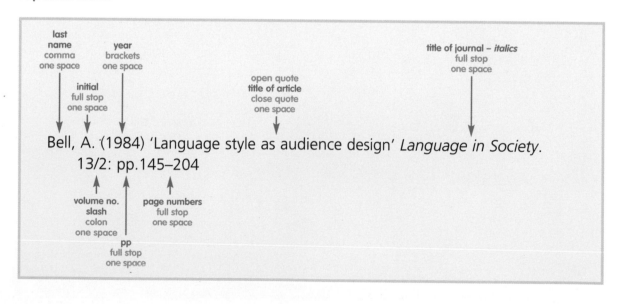

A section or chapter of a book

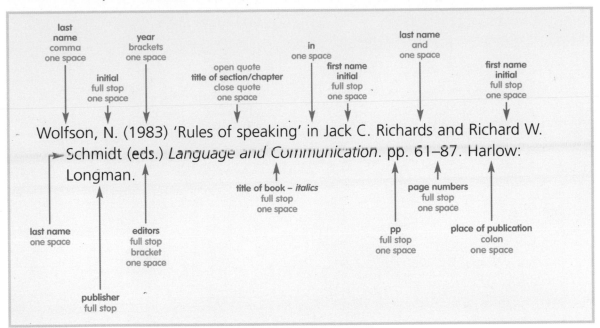

An internet site

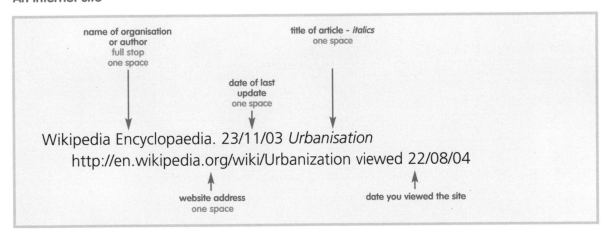